LET FAITH HELP YOU HEAL

Put God's Healing Power to Work for You

Publications International, Ltd.

Anne Broyles is a United Methodist minister, writer, and retreat leader. Her numerous books in the Christian devotional field include *Journaling: A Spiritual Journey, Growing Together in Love: God Known Through Family Life,* and *Meeting God Through Worship.* Broyles is married and the mother of two young adult children. She lives in New England where she works as a faith relations coordinator for Habitat for Humanity.

Cover photo: Oxford Scientific/Photolibrary

Unless otherwise noted, all Scripture quotations are taken from the *New Revised Standard Version* of the Bible. Copyright © 1989 by the Division of Christian Education of the National Council of the Churches of Christ in the U.S.A. Used by permission. All rights reserved.

Scripture quotations marked The Message are from *The Message.* Copyright © 1993, 1994, 1995 by Eugene H. Peterson. Used by permission of NavPress Publishing Group. All rights reserved.

Scriptures marked CEV are taken from the *Contemporary English Version* of the Bible. Copyright © 1995 by American Bible Society. Used by permission.

Copyright © 2008 Publications International, Ltd. All rights reserved. This book may not be reproduced or quoted in whole or in part by any means whatsoever without written permission from:

Louis Weber, CEO
Publications International, Ltd.
7373 North Cicero Avenue
Lincolnwood, Illinois 60712

Permission is never granted for commercial purposes.

ISBN-13: 978-1-4127-1619-2
ISBN-10: 1-4127-1619-5

Manufactured in U.S.A.

8 7 6 5 4 3 2 1

Contents

Getting Healthy and Whole ✦ 4

Chapter One
Believe in God's Power to Heal You ✦ 7

Chapter Two
Envision Yourself Whole ✦ 26

Chapter Three
Begin Your Healing Process
with Forgiveness ✦ 47

Chapter Four
Forgive Yourself and Allow God
to Transform Your Life ✦ 64

Chapter Five
Let Go of That Which Binds You ✦ 84

Chapter Six
Realize That You Are a
Wounded Healer ✦ 103

Chapter Seven
Thank God for Your New Life ✦ 122

Chapter Eight
Focus on an Intimate and Vibrant
Relationship with God ✦ 141

Getting Healthy and Whole

WHEN YOU SCRAPED an elbow as a child, did you run to your mother and ask her to "kiss it and make it all better"? As children, most of us thought that pain was no worse than an occasional cut or scrape. Serious illness, death, and the need for healing did not enter our minds.

But after we reached adulthood, we became more aware of the deeper issues associated with pain and illness. We became more aware of loved ones who had to deal with serious physical or emotional difficulties. We realized that some hurts are too deep for the "kiss it and make it all better" solution. As people of faith, however, we also know God offers us a new life in a variety of ways. A cancer patient experiences remission. An abused woman finds strength to walk away from a destructive relationship. A heroin addict successfully completes a detox program. Each of those people experiences the physical, emotional, or spiritual healing they need.

What might healing look like in your life? How might you envision yourself as healthy and whole? This book will help you believe in God's power to heal you. It will encourage you to begin your healing process by forgiving yourself and others. God can transform your life in unexpected ways if you let go of all that binds you and prevents you from living as a healthy and whole person. As the World Health Organization stated, "Health is a state of complete physical, mental and social well-being, and not merely the absence of disease or infirmity."

Once you're on the path to healing, you may realize how all that has wounded you in the past (illness, relationships, abuse) enables you to help others in their healing process. You can give thanks for the fresh start God offers you by renewing and strengthening your relationship with him.

What cannot be questioned is God's willingness to heal and the provision He has already made for that purpose to be fulfilled.

Colin Urquhart

~~~~~~~~~~

In Deuteronomy 30:19, God says through Moses, "I call heaven and earth to witness against you today that I have set before you life and death, blessings and curses. Choose life so that you and your descendants may live."

God wants you to be healthy and happy, to choose life and blessings instead of death and curses. We hope that this book will provide the encouragement and resources you need to live in life's fullness. As Marcus Valerius Martial wrote, "Life is not merely to be alive, but to be well." May this book guide you toward wellness and new life.

Believe in God's Power to Heal You

*Sometimes a light surprises the
Christian while he sings;*

*It is the Lord, who rises with
healing in His wings:*

*When comforts are declining,
He grants the soul again*

*A season of clear shining,
to cheer it after rain.*

William Cowper

WHAT'S YOUR USUAL ANSWER when someone asks, "How are you?" Does "fine" always mean "healthy, happy and strong"? Or does that pat response also cover the days when you feel vulnerable, afraid, depressed; when your sciatica is acting up, or you're worried about a cancer test; when you're boiling over with rage or ready to burst into tears?

Most of us are skilled at presenting ourselves as "fine." Just looking at a person's outside, you can't know: Does she feel healthy and whole? Or is he wounded, sick, and in need of healing physically, spiritually, or emotionally?

> *It's no coincidence that four of the six letters in health are "heal."*
>
> Ed Northstrum

Contemporary medicine continues to make enormous advances in preventing and healing disease. Yet many of us live compromised lives: We are not as healthy in body, mind, and spirit as we could and should be. We assume we must live with physical pain. Our relationships are strained at best, ruptured at worst. Our worries keep us up at night. Some aspect of our lives needs healing.

"Health," "whole," "healing," and "holy" all derive from the same Old English word root, *hal*. If we are healthy, we are whole, healed, and holy:

mind, body, and spirit. If one part of our life is out of balance, our total health is compromised.

Which of these definitions of "whole" describe you? Which of those would you like to describe you?

___ healthy
___ unhurt
___ healed
___ complete
___ restored
___ intact
___ unimpaired

There's good news for any of us who want to be "whole." The God who made us and loves us desires wholeness for us. Jesus said, "I came that they may have life, and have it abundantly" (John 10:10). Jesus' offer of abundant life includes wholeness and healing.

~~~~~~~~~~

O Thou who art the Way, the Truth, and the Life, we lift our hearts to Thee.
Guide us in the Way this day, enlighten us with

— Let Faith Help You Heal —

the Truth, and grant us the more abundant Life which Thou alone canst give.
This we ask, not that we may selfishly get good or glory for ourselves, but that we may do good unto others and so glorify Thy name.

—Howard Grose

~~~~~~~~~~

Cassandra was a successful CEO of her own small company. For years she suffered from chronic back pain, a condition that often interfered with her work, but she stoically hid her problem as best she could. She worked long hours and had little time to dwell on the condition or take the steps her doctor recommended to strengthen her back and alleviate pain. One day, one of Cassandra's employees found her bent over her desk unable to straighten up.

"It's just a hitch in my back," the boss explained.

The employee pressed for more details and asked what Cassandra was doing about her pain.

"I can live with it," Cassandra said.

"But why would you want to? Don't you want to be healed?"

That question started Cassandra on a spiritual journey that led to her healing. She prayed that her pain might go away. She made a doctor's appointment to talk seriously about action she could take to strengthen her back. She took time to become more physically fit. In time, Cassandra was healed not only of her back pain but also of her need to always appear strong and invincible. She decided it was okay to ask for and receive help. She joined an intercessory prayer group at her church so she could pray for the healing of other people, as well as for her own release from suffering. Her emotional "letting go" paralleled the physical "letting go" or easing of her back pain.

To be "whole" is to be spiritually, emotionally, and physically healthy.

Colin Urquhart

⸺ Let Faith Help You Heal ⸺

Ekaterina ("Katia") Alexandrovna Gordeeva and her husband, Sergei Grinkov, charmed the world as they won Olympic gold medals and other championship titles in pairs skating. The two skated together from the time they were 10 and 14. They fell in love long after their partnership on ice began and married in 1991. Their daughter, Daria, was born in 1992. Katia and Sergei won their second Olympic gold medal in 1994 and were inducted into the World Figure Skating Hall of Fame. Professionally and personally, life was good.

Then, in 1995, Sergei collapsed and died from a massive heart attack at age 28. Katia was suddenly a widow with a young child. How could she go on without her skating partner and the love of her life? The pain of loss needed healing. Like anyone who loses a loved one, Katia needed time and the support of good friends to ease through the pain to new life.

The first time Katia skated after her husband's death, she said, "To come back on the ice was hard, and at the same time it was kind of a healing process." Healing continued as Katia returned to figure skating, wrote a book called *My Sergei: A Love Story*, remarried, and had a second daughter. Although her life is not as she had envisioned it when she fell in love with Sergei, Katia is happy and fulfilled, having experienced healing from her grief.

For everything there is a season, and a time for every matter under heaven:
a time to be born, and a time to die;
a time to plant, and a time to pluck up what is planted;
a time to kill, and a time to heal;
a time to break down, and a time to build up;
a time to weep, and a time to laugh;
a time to mourn, and a time to dance;
a time to throw away stones, and a time to gather stones together;
a time to embrace, and a time to refrain from embracing;
a time to seek, and a time to lose;
a time to keep, and a time to throw away;
a time to tear, and a time to sew;
a time to keep silence, and a time to speak;
a time to love, and a time to hate;
a time for war, and a time for peace.

—Ecclesiastes 3:1–8

The New Testament is full of examples of how Jesus healed a variety of people with different sorts of ailments. As Mark records it, "And wherever he went, into villages or cities or farms, they laid the sick in the marketplaces, and begged him that they might touch even the fringe of his cloak; and all who touched it were healed" (Mark 6:56).

Jesus healed a leper who came to him and said, "Lord, if you choose, you can make me clean" (Matthew 8:2). When a soldier asked to have his servant healed from paralysis and pain, the man said, "Only speak the word, and my servant will be healed" (verse 8). A religious leader named Jairus pleaded with Jesus to heal his daughter, saying, "Come and lay your hands on her, so that she may be made well, and live" (Mark 5:23). A woman who had suffered from bleeding for 12 years touched Jesus' cloak: "If I but touch his clothes I will be made well" (verse 28).

Let Faith Help You Heal

What do you notice about these stories of healing? In each case, someone believed that Jesus had the power to perform the healing. They came to him because they needed his help. And although the healings happened in different ways, not only did Jesus use his power to heal and change the lives of the people he healed, but anyone watching the event would have been affected in some way, as well.

Health is a state of complete harmony of the body, mind and spirit. When one is free from physical disabilities and mental distractions, the gates of the soul open.

B.K.S. Iyengar

Dear God,
Help my unbelief.
When I'm in pain, I forget that you care about me.
I forget that you have helped me through my trials.
I forget that you hold me in your arms to keep me safe.
I forget that you are feeling my pain with me.
I forget that you love me,

Let Faith Help You Heal

I forget that I am important to you.
Show me your presence—let me feel your
    enveloping love.
Heal my hurting soul.
Thank you for staying with me even in my unbelief.
Amen.

~~~~~~~~

Hippocrates, "the father of medicine," wrote, "Healing is a matter of time, but it is sometimes also a matter of opportunity." The people who came to Jesus took the opportunity to ask for his help, touch his cloak, express their faith. In many cases, Jesus responded to the person with a variation of "Your faith has made you well" (sometimes, "Your faith has made you whole"). In other words, his power to heal responded to their faith as well as to their need for healing.

The story of the healing of blind Bartimaeus illustrates both the deep desire to be healed and Jesus' appreciation of the faith that made healing possible:

"They came to Jericho. As he and his disciples and a large crowd were leaving Jericho, Bartimaeus son of Timaeus, a blind beggar, was sitting by the roadside. When he heard that it was Jesus of Nazareth, he began to shout out and say, 'Jesus, Son of David, have mercy on me!' Many sternly ordered him to be quiet, but he cried out even more loudly, 'Son of David, have mercy on me!' Jesus stood still and said, 'Call him here.' And they called the blind man, saying to him, 'Take heart; get up, he is calling you.' So throwing off his cloak, he sprang up and came to Jesus. Then Jesus said to him, 'What do you want me to do for you?' The blind man said to him, 'My teacher, let me see again.' Jesus said to him, 'Go; your faith has made you well.' Immediately he regained his sight and followed him on the way" (Mark 10:46–52).

Bartimaeus didn't speak in grand, theological terms. He didn't post his credentials or give Jesus a list of reasons why he should be healed from his blindness. Bartimaeus had probably heard stories about Jesus. His interest was piqued: If Jesus healed others, could he heal me, too? Bartimaeus sat by the side of the road, begging (because of his disability, probably the only means of earning money he had). When he realized Jesus was coming his way, he began to shout. At that point in the story, he didn't ask for healing. He just wanted to get Jesus' attention.

Given the crowds and the noise, it was remarkable that Jesus heard one man's entreaties, but he stood still and asked the blind man to come to him. Bartimaeus took a literal step toward Jesus, who asked him, "What do you want me to do for you?" At Bartimaeus's response, Jesus said, "Your faith has made you well." The once-blind man left his old life behind and joined Jesus on his journey.

What can we learn from Bartimaeus? First, if we desire healing, we can come to Jesus and ask for help. Second, we must trust that Jesus will hear us and respond.

Let Faith Help You Heal

Bartimaeus's prayer has long been used as the "Prayer of the Heart." Developed and practiced in Russia, the simple words "Lord Jesus Christ, have mercy on me, a sinner" can be repeated throughout the day. Some people find it helpful to use the rhythm of their own inhale/exhale pattern as a breath prayer. You might want to try repeating this Prayer of the Heart. Take quiet time alone. Focus on your breath pattern, breathing deeply, then begin to repeat as follows:

> Inhale: Lord Jesus Christ,
> Exhale: Have mercy on me, a sinner.
> (Repeat.)

When we ask for healing, we are not giving God orders. We are asking God to be with us and work in us. As Tilda Norburg and Robert D. Webber wrote, "Prayer is not directing God but directing ourselves toward God: not informing God, but conforming ourselves to God . . . the heart of healing prayer is discerning how God is working for healing in a particular situation, and conforming our prayers to the movement of God's Spirit. This is not magic, but it is mystery, the mystery of entering into communion with God through the Holy Spirit."

The greatest wealth is health.
Virgil

Even those who dedicate their lives to medicine can't fully explain how and why healing works. Norman Cousins, writer and Adjunct Professor of Medical Humanities for the School of Medicine at the University of California, said, "It is reasonable to expect the doctor to recognize that science may not have all the answers to problems of health and healing."

In a 1995 Dartmouth Medical study, open-heart surgery patients who found comfort in their faith were three times more likely to be alive six months after their surgery. Herbert Benson, a

Harvard cardiologist, said, "I am astonished that my scientific studies have so conclusively shown that our bodies are wired to (be) nourished and healed by prayer and other exercises of belief."

What do you think? Can faith in God heal? Have you been healed or know someone who was healed? Just because Jesus healed people 2,000 years ago, does that mean you can be healed today?

Dozens of medical studies have shown that people who rely on God heal more quickly. That doesn't mean that someone who does not get well is spiritually bankrupt. Much of healing remains a mystery, so it makes no sense to pass judgment on an individual who dies of cancer or can't shake mental illness. Jesus was clear about not comparing ourselves with or passing judgment on other people. "Do not judge, so that you may not be judged. For with the judgment you make you will be judged, and the measure you give will be the measure you get" (Matthew 7:1–2).

Focus on yourself, not others. What in your life needs healing? Is there a physical ailment that you no longer want to live with? Are you struggling with addictions that prevent you from living the abundant life Jesus promised? Do you have relationships that are painful and need to be healed? Is there a sorrow that weighs you down?

He took the punishment, and that made us whole.
Through his bruises we get healed.

Isaiah 53:5 (The Message)

You picked up this book called *Let Faith Help You Heal*. Chances are there's some part of your life that you hope for healing, whether you have admitted it to others or only yourself. Or you may know someone who needs healing. At the very least, you may be intrigued by the possibility of healing in your life or the world.

Let Faith Help You Heal

"Come to me," Jesus says. "What do you want me to do for you?"

Take a few minutes to think about this question. Then if you feel ready, read the following prayers and decide if you feel ready to pray one of them or to form your own prayer.

Here I am, Jesus. You know me
    better than I know myself.
You understand even the parts of
    me I don't understand.
So, like Bartimaeus, I stand before you,
Daring to shout, "Son of David, have mercy on me!"
And here you are, listening to me.
"Come to me," you say. "What do you
    want me to do for you?"
I gather courage to answer your question.
Jesus, I need you to _____.
I believe you can help me.
I trust that you will provide
    resources for my healing.
I am ready to do what I need to do to be healed.
Amen.

Gracious God,
I know you love me.
I know you want the best for me.
As I come before you today, you
    know my aches and pains,

The things that hurt my body and the
   things that pain my soul.
I ask that you heal me in whatever way I need
   healing.
Open me to the power of your love.
Help me accept the healing you offer.
And let me rest gently in the palm of your hand
As a baby rests in its mother's arms.
In your name, I pray.
Amen.

Lord,
I manage fine.
I'm healthy enough.
Yet I'm intrigued.
I'm trying to be open to the possibility that you
   might be able to heal me in some wonderful way
   I can't even dream of.
I'm ready to explore this further.
I don't know where it will lead, but I know you'll be
   with me on this journey.
Thank you for accepting me as I am, unbelief and all.
Amen.

~~~~~~~~~~

Perhaps as you read the prayers, some of the words stuck in your throat. You may feel like saying, "I'm not sure about this healing business. I need time to think about what healing might mean for me." Or you feel skeptical that healing is possible. We live in a world that emphasizes science and technology, what can be seen and proven. Yet there is much in life that science and technology cannot explain. The man given two months to live is healthy 20 years later. The brain-damaged child learns to walk and talk despite the original prognosis. "Although the world is full of suffering," Helen Keller said, "it is also full of the overcoming of it."

Asking for healing is a bold act. You may not feel ready to pray these words. And that's fine. Use your time while reading this book as a time of discernment, of looking inward and assessing where you are in your life. You might learn something new about yourself. And you might end up accepting the abundant life that Jesus promised.

Envision Yourself Whole

Wholeness is a gift that comes to us gradually through the process of daily living with God.

Marjorie Thompson

Gabe served several tours of duty during the Vietnam War. At the war's onset, he was a fresh-faced 18-year-old. By the time he came home, Gabe had seen too much killing. Years later he still awoke most nights screaming from nightmares that relived the battle at Hill 882. He'd had the dream so often that he tried to wake himself before the napalm hit and fire engulfed his buddies in the dream. Living through that once had been bad enough.

"Put it behind you," his father told him. "That war's long past."

Let Faith Help You Heal

Gabe couldn't escape the trauma inflicted by his years in 'Nam. He escaped into drug addiction and had trouble keeping a job. One bleak day 22 years after his return from Vietnam, a doctor at the VA Hospital got his attention with a question: "Do you want to be healthy again?"

Gabe bristled, then heard the question echo inside him. Within a month he had signed up for a weekly support group. To his surprise, Gabe found it helpful to share memories he'd long repressed. He began attending the church in which he'd grown up. The sights and sounds of mass brought him comfort. Yes, he thought. Yes, I want to be healthy again.

For people who have experienced trauma or sorrow or physical pain, it can be difficult to imagine what health and wholeness might be like. Good health may require changes for which they may not feel ready. For instance, once he claimed his desire to be healthy again, Gabe had to face the challenge of conquering his addiction. He had to reenter the job market and reestablish relationships with people from whom he'd cut himself off. He knew the changes would lead to a better life, but change required his effort and energy. And who knew what might happen after change occurred?

> *Diseases of the soul are more dangerous and more numerous than those of the body.*
> Cicero

Jesus understood that healing wasn't simply a moment in time; healing was a process that would continue as the healed person lived out his or her new beginning. "After this there was a festival of the Jews, and Jesus went up to Jerusalem. Now in Jerusalem by the Sheep Gate there is a pool, called in Hebrew Beth-zatha, which has five porticoes. In these lay many invalids—blind, lame, and paralyzed. One man was there who had been ill for 38 years. When Jesus saw him lying there and knew that he had been there a long time, he said to him, 'Do you want to be made well?' The sick man answered him, 'Sir, I have no one to put me into the pool when the water is stirred up; and while I am making my way, someone else steps down ahead of me.' Jesus said to him, 'Stand up, take your mat and walk.' At once the man was made well, and he took up his mat and began to walk" (John 5:1–8).

"Do you want to be made well?" What a penetrating question! Wouldn't anyone who had suffered for 38 years desire healing? Yet what would come after healing was unknown, as new life always is, and sometimes we're afraid of what we don't know. The sick man knew what it was like to live with physical infirmity, to wait for healing, and to depend on others. Wholeness was the unknown. How would other people respond to him? Could he make a living?

When Jesus said, "Stand up, take your mat and walk," he challenged the invalid to give up being cared for by other people and make a new life for himself. Rather than responding, "Are you crazy? I just told you: I can't even get into the healing waters of this pool by myself!" the ill man accepted Jesus' gift of healing. He stood and walked.

> *Vision looks inward and becomes duty. Vision looks outward and becomes aspiration. Vision looks upward and becomes faith.*
>
> Stephen S. Wise

"Do you want to be made well?" If we answer "Yes," we must be ready to take that first step. How do we imagine our lives might be different if we were healed? What action are we willing to take to achieve wholeness? Before we can grasp the healing that is possible, we need to create a healthy vision of ourselves—body, mind, and spirit.

↽ Let Faith Help You Heal ↼

At the age of 30, fighting breast and cervical cancer with chemotherapy after major surgeries, Marion Luna Brem was given two to five years to live. Her medical insurance ran out, and the family was left with huge bills that left them in debt. Because of the emotional and financial strain, her husband left her, and Brem had to support two young children. Despite the fact that she had little education or job experience, Brem believed she had unique ideas for marketing automobiles to women. She tried 17 car dealerships before she found one willing to take her on. By the end of her first year, she was "Salesperson of the Year" because of her perseverance and her ability to envision a new future for herself.

Brem continued to work in car sales and eventually financed her own dealership. Today, almost 25 years after she found herself cancer-ridden, abandoned by her husband, and without full-time employment, Marion Luna Brem is cancer-free and owns two car dealerships, an ad agency, and a real estate company. "Courage is not a gift, courage is a decision," she says.

Part of the healing process is taking responsibility for our lives and health. Jesus is not a fairy godmother who zaps us with a magic wand: "Poof! You're healed!" You may know people who complain about their ailments, but they refuse to take action for a healthier life. The person with emphysema or lung cancer continues to smoke. The diabetic doesn't follow a healthy diet. The manic-depressive takes her medication sporadically. Those who choose to live healthy lives are more likely to act responsibly and practice healthy living as much as possible.

An old nursery rhyme says,

> The best six doctors anywhere
> And no one can deny it
> Are sunshine, water, rest, and air
> Exercise and diet.
> These six will gladly you attend

Let Faith Help You Heal

> If only you are willing
> Your mind they'll ease
> Your will they'll mend
> And charge you not a shilling.

Health experts are not in complete agreement about what constitutes a healthy lifestyle, but most agree that there are general practices that lead to healthy living. Some of them even correlate with the nursery rhyme's wisdom! How would you rate your health practices? Using the list below, take an inventory of your life. Rate yourself on a scale of 1 to 5, with 1 being NEVER and 5 being ALWAYS.

1. I am physically active and get moderate exercise every day.
2. I surround myself with people who are nurturing and positive.
3. I include at least 6–10 servings of fruits and vegetables in my daily diet.
4. I find ways to connect with God on a regular basis through prayer or worship.

⇜Let Faith Help You Heal⇝

5. I try to balance the time I spend working and relaxing.
6. I eat a low-fat, high-fiber, healthy diet.
7. I regularly take time to enjoy God's beautiful natural creation.
8. I drink plenty of water.
9. I get enough sleep every night.
10. I only drink alcohol in moderation.

Add your score. If 50 represents a person who takes his or her health seriously, are you where you would like to be? Are there any areas in which you might need to make some changes? Say you don't get much exercise. Making a change doesn't mean you run a marathon tomorrow. Perhaps you begin with a daily walk—15 minutes, 30 minutes, whatever you can manage. Build up to more physical activity according to your doctor's recommendations. Or if you spend most of your time indoors, what parks, gardens, or beaches are near enough that you might schedule time to appreciate God's creation?

Let Faith Help You Heal

You may have noticed that some of the things on the list are about physical health (diet and nutrition, sleep), others pertain to emotional health (nurturing and positive friends), and some about spiritual health (connecting with God in prayer, worship, nature). Remember how the root word for "health," "whole," "healing," and "holy" all derive from the same Old English word root? Health and healing involve the mind, body, and spirit. When you think about the list on pages 33–34, which area(s) of your health do you feel are most in balance: mind, body, or spirit?

Full health begins with our vision of ourselves as healthy and whole: strong bodies, strong spirits, strong minds. Consider the list, and write down the top three ways you consistently work on health and wholeness.

1. _____
2. _____
3. _____

Let Faith Help You Heal

Now write down three things you would like to improve upon, health-wise.

1. _____

2. _____

3. _____

In order to move toward a healthier, whole life, what might you need? From the following checklist, choose what applies to you.

In order to move toward a healthier, whole life I would need...

___ A caring community of people who love me and nurture me.
___ Education on nutrition and eating healthily.
___ Regular physical exercise.
___ To be gentle with myself.
___ More focused time with God.
___ New ways to relax.
___ More time for myself.

Let Faith Help You Heal

___ To let go of some bad habits, such as:
_____
_____

___ To forgive myself and others.
___ Confidence in my ability to change.
___ Freedom from a destructive relationship.
___ A support group for my specific goals (such as a hiking group, a weight-loss program, a church prayer group, or Alcoholics Anonymous).
___ To go to bed earlier.
___ To let go of my painful past.
___ A less stressful job.
___ To change my expectations.

___ _____
___ _____
___ _____

In the spaces on the next page, write your vision for how your life might look if you were healthy in body, mind, and spirit. If one or more of these areas already feels healthy, great! It's still good to keep the vision of wholeness before us so we can stay on track.

Healthy body:
_____
_____
_____
_____
_____
_____

Healthy mind:
_____
_____
_____
_____
_____
_____

Healthy spirit:
_____
_____

Let Faith Help You Heal

_____
_____
_____

Now put those three components together in one short statement, which will serve as your Healing Vision Statement.

_____
_____

Wondrous God,
I praise your name.
Your Word is life.
I believe you can heal me.
Be with me when I am sick,
And remind me to praise you when I am well.
Thank you for healing me in the past,
And for future healing.
Keep me in good health
That I might serve you
And praise your name.
Amen.

"The wish for healing has always been half of health," wrote Lucius Annaeus Seneca. In other words, after we envision ourselves whole, we have to desire healing. We have to answer "Yes!" to the question: "Do you want to be made well?" Once we commit to wholeness and healing, we enter a process that continues as we live out our new beginning. We don't know exactly what our healing may look like, but we have confidence that God will work in us to bring about whatever changes are needed.

Take a 3×5 index card or other sturdy paper, and write out your vision. Then post it in a place you can regularly see it to be reminded of the health and wholeness you desire. Or write out Jesus' question: "Do you want to be made well?" and post it on your bathroom mirror, refrigerator door, or other easy-to-notice place. You could also write some sort of code word like "Health," "Wholeness," or "Envision Wellness."

Although you may know what sort of wellness you want for your life, only God knows how to give you what you need. Think of how parents provide for their children. "I want to eat the whole bag of candy!" and "Buy me every toy in the store!" are children's requests for what they think they need, but few parents fulfill those requests in the way demanded. Because of their age and life experience and out of love, parents know that what the child most needs is not a belly full of candy or a room full of toys, but a nurturing love that provides more fulfillment than material possessions.

"Ask, and it will be given you; search, and you will find; knock, and the door will be opened for you. For everyone who asks receives, and everyone who searches finds, and for everyone who knocks, the door will be opened. Is there anyone among you who, if your child asks for bread, will give a stone? Or if the child asks for a fish, will give a snake? If you then, who are evil, know how to give good gifts to your children, how much more will your Father in heaven give good things to those who ask him!" (Matthew 7:7–11).

~Let Faith Help You Heal~

Even as we ask for healing and trust that God will work in our lives, we know that God is in charge. He is the Loving Parent who sees the big picture of which we understand only a part. If the healing we want doesn't happen on our time schedule, we know that, as Max Lucado said, "Though you hear nothing, He is speaking. Though you see nothing, He is acting. With God there are no accidents. Every incident is intended to bring us closer to Him."

Why are you down in the dumps, dear soul?
Why are you crying the blues?
Fix my eyes on God—
soon I'll be praising again.
He puts a smile on my face.
He's my God.

Psalm 42:11 (The Message)

In their book, *Stretch Out Your Hand: Exploring Healing Prayer,* Tilda Norburg and Robert D. Webber write, "We need to trust the healing process Jesus offers and to understand that being healed does not always mean being cured. Whenever we open ourselves to God's healing, some kind of healing takes place, though it may not be in the way we expect."

Now, this may not be what you want to hear. Most of us would like to give God a list of wishes to grant with our deadline for completion of the assignment. Our Big Picture God, however, may have a different method and timeline for us. Healing may come in a form we cannot anticipate. We have to trust God: "For surely I know the plans I have for you, says the Lord, plans for your welfare and not for harm, to give you a future with hope" (Jeremiah 29:11).

I believe that God is in me as the sun is in the color and fragrance of a flower—the light in my darkness, the Voice in my Silence.

Helen Keller

⇠ Let Faith Help You Heal ⇢

Athlete Gail Devers set a U.S. record in the 100-meter hurdles during her senior year at UCLA. As a top athlete, Devers was training for the 1988 Olympics when she was diagnosed with Graves' disease. Her health so deteriorated that doctors considered amputating both of her feet. At that point, some people might have doubted God, but Devers believed in "Let go and let God." As she says, "With lots of hard work, determination, perseverance and faith in God, I was able to resume training and regain my health."

Seventeen months later, Devers won her first Olympic gold medal in Barcelona. Devers continued her running career and won seven championship titles, including another gold medal at the 1996 Olympic games in Atlanta. Today she is a motivational speaker who still practices the "Let go and let God" faith that made her a champion.

"If I had my life to live over, I would ask for Graves' disease again. It made me the person that I am, and I like who I am. It showed me the value of faith and determination. When the doctors told me I might not walk again, my faith told me I could."

God of the strong and the weak,
The brave and the fearful,
I come before you to place myself in your loving hands.
Take my broken places and make them whole.
Heal my wounds that I might be strong for you.
Give me patience to accept your timing,
And help me to trust in your goodness.
In your gracious name, I pray. Amen.

When we envision ourselves as whole, we hold on to that vision even when we may temporarily not feel as whole in body, mind, or spirit as we would like. As Devers says, "Remember all things are possible for those who believe."

By creating your own vision for wholeness, you've taken a giant step. In the next chapter, you'll find out how you can begin your healing process with forgiveness. For now, please take some quiet time to remind yourself of Isaiah's comforting words:

Let Faith Help You Heal

Have you not known? Have you not heard?
The Lord is the everlasting God,
    the Creator of the ends of the earth.
He does not faint or grow weary;
    his understanding is unsearchable.
He gives power to the faint,
    and strengthens the powerless.
Even youths will faint and be weary,
    and the young will fall exhausted;
but those who wait for the Lord shall renew their strength,
    they shall mount up with wings like eagles,
they shall run and not be weary,
    they shall walk and not faint.

—Isaiah 40:28–31

Begin Your Healing Process with Forgiveness

It is by forgiving that one is forgiven.

Mother Teresa

As a child, Kate responded to any perceived offense by withholding her affection. "I'd just stop talking to my parents, my brother, my friends," she said. When she was angry and pouting because she thought she had been wronged, her family tried everything to make her happy. "What they didn't realize was that I *liked* being angry," Kate explained. "I felt most powerful when I was mad. Watching my parents and brother scurry around to cheer me up made me feel loved." Eventually, the angry girl matured and became secure enough in her family's love that she no longer needed to be angry to feel loved. Most important, she learned to forgive.

After the death of his father, Henry began to suffer from debilitating panic attacks. He assumed his sadness somehow caused the attacks, but in a class at his church on "The Way of Forgiveness," Henry faced the truth and experienced a powerful letting-go of the fury he had long repressed toward his father. "I didn't want to recognize all the ways my father had abused me over the years," he said. "His death somehow released the anger and negativity leftover from my unhappy childhood. Others in the class encouraged me to forgive my father so I could move on." Within a month, Henry's panic attacks subsided.

Forgiveness says yes to life, hope, the future.

Marjorie J. Thompson

As Kate and Henry's stories show, our anger is often rooted in hurt and fear. We may not feel loved and appreciated. We may have suffered another person's cruelty or abandonment. We feel justified in our anger and disinclined to offer forgiveness to someone who has hurt us.

You and I may find it difficult to forgive even the small things those around us unwittingly do to offend us. A neighbor is unfriendly. A friend divulges one of our secrets. A spouse forgets an anniversary. We can choose to fume and let our anger become a wall between us and the person we feel has done us wrong, or we can choose to let go of our anger and forgive.

> *Forgiveness comes to us as a gift, often when we feel least worthy of receiving it.... It can be accepted or rejected. What we do with it is up to us.*
>
> Johann C. Arnold

Henri J. M. Nouwen wrote, "Forgiveness is the name of love practiced among people who love poorly." We want to be loving in everything we do, but our humanness gets in the way. It's hard to love unconditionally! It's difficult to offer forgiveness in all situations.

"The fuel of bitterness is always expended in vain," according to Johann C. Arnold, "but the love of a forgiving heart is never wasted." How do you want to use your energy? In anger and bitterness, or in freedom and reconciliation?

Think of the worst thing you have done in your life to hurt another person. If they forgave you, how did that feel? If they have not yet forgiven you, how does it feel? Forgiveness often provides release from bondage, a new beginning, a chance for a fresh start.

> *One who forgives an affront*
> *fosters friendship,*
> *but one who dwells on disputes*
> *will alienate a friend.*
>
> **Proverbs 17:9**

Jesus spoke strong words about forgiveness: "For if you forgive others their trespasses, your heavenly Father will also forgive you; but if you do not forgive others, neither will your Father forgive your trespasses" (Matthew 6:14–15). That's plain enough! Our own need for forgiveness depends on our ability to get past whatever in us cannot offer forgiveness to others. We may want to counter: I'm forgiving most of the time. Isn't there a limit on this forgiveness business? How many times do I have to forgive? Even a disciple who walked and talked with Jesus had the same question.

"Then Peter came and said to [Jesus], 'Lord, if another member of the church sins against me, how often should I forgive? As many as seven times?' Jesus said to him, 'Not seven times, but, I tell you, seventy-seven times'" (Matthew 18:21–22). To emphasize the point, Jesus told a parable about a king who had pity on one of his servants, releasing him and forgiving him a huge debt.

That forgiven servant, however, did not act out of the grace given him. Instead, he had another servant thrown into prison when he couldn't pay back a small debt. When the king discovered the servant's mean-spirited behavior toward the second servant, he said, "You wicked slave! I forgave you all that debt because you pleaded with me. Should you not have had mercy on your fellow slave, as I had mercy on you?" (verses 32–33). The king then severely punished the first servant.

> *Count yourself lucky, how happy you must be—you get a fresh start, your slate's wiped clean.*
>
> Psalm 32:1 (The Message)

Jesus used the parable of the unforgiving servant to make a point: "So my heavenly Father will also do to every one of you, if you do not forgive your brother or sister from your heart" (verse 35). Or, in the words of an old folk saying, "He who cannot forgive breaks the bridge over which he himself must pass."

There are many reasons to forgive others and let go of our anger. The only reason to hold on to that negativity and withhold forgiveness is that we may feel it gives us power over the other person. Righteous anger is a wall that keeps us in and others out. The Buddha spoke to this when he said, "Holding on to anger is like grasping a hot coal with the intent of throwing it at someone else—you are the one who gets burned."

The practice of forgiveness is our most important contribution to the healing of the world.

Marianne Williamson

When we hold a grudge against another person, we hold ourselves prisoner. Freedom can come only through our willingness to offer forgiveness to a person who may very well deserve our anger.

We forgive them for our own sake as well as for theirs. "In this life...we are unable to forget whatever remains unforgiven," Guy Finley wrote. "So, if we won't let go of some pain—whose time is now past—then who is to blame for the weight of this burden still being carried on our back?"

Only a free person can live with an uneven score.

Lewis B. Smedes

But how can I forget the wrong that was done me? Forgiveness does not necessarily mean forgetting, but rather, living in full connection with a person whose past hurtful action is no longer pertinent to the present.

God,
You said we should, "Forgive us our sins as we forgive those who sin against us."
Do you realize how hard that can be?
When I've been hurt, my anger and resentment feels justified.

Let Faith Help You Heal

Yet I know that my lack of forgiveness hurts me as much as it hurts the one who hurt me.
I need your help with forgiveness.
Help me forgive anyone who has ever wounded me, however slight or great the hurt.
Forgive me both the offenses I did on purpose and the ways I hurt others without realizing it.
Whenever possible, let me know how to make amends to those I have hurt.
Help me accept forgiveness from others and graciously offer my own forgiveness.
From now on, guide me in a way of living that respects other people and seeks to understand rather than to condemn their actions.
For this is the way that leads to life. Amen.

~~~~~~~

When Sue Norton's father and his wife were murdered in a home robbery, she was devastated. As she sat through the trial of B. K. Knighton, the young man accused of the killing, she realized she did not hate him the way others present in the courtroom seemed to hate him. Just before the trial ended, Sue spent a sleepless night in prayer. The words "Sue, you don't have to hate B. K., you could forgive him" came to her. She asked permission to visit the prisoner in his cell while the jury deliberated his case. "I didn't think of him as killer. I thought of him as a human being," she said.

Few understood her decision to forgive the man who had murdered two members of her family. "There is no way to heal and get over the trauma without forgiveness," Sue believes. "You must forgive and forget and get on with your life. That is what Jesus would do."

While B. K. was on death row prior to his execution and since, Sue has been active in Murder Victims Families for Reconciliation and the Kansas Coalition to Abolish the Death Penalty.

When we are victims of radical evil, we are not asked to forgive the evil act. We are asked to remember that the perpetrator, even though trapped for now in evil, is nonetheless a child of God.

Flora Slosson Wuellner

~LET FAITH HELP YOU HEAL~

Corrie ten Boom's story is a wonderful example of how God can work in us even when we may not feel like forgiving. Corrie grew up in a strong Christian home in the Netherlands. When the Nazis invaded their nation, the ten Booms joined the underground movement and hid Jewish refugees in attic rooms of their home. In 1944, all three ten Booms were arrested and taken to the Ravensbruck concentration camp, where they led Bible studies and shared their faith. During her imprisonment, Corrie promised God that if she survived, she would spread the message of God's love and forgiveness. Her father and sister died, but because of an administrative error, Corrie was released from Ravensbruck.

Corrie dedicated the rest of her life to preaching, writing, and speaking about God's love. Her book, *The Hiding Place*, told her story. Years after the war ended, a former Ravensbruck S.S. guard came up to Corrie after she spoke at a worship service. Corrie recognized him, but he did not recognize her. He explained that he had been a camp guard during the war but that after the war he had become a Christian. He said he felt that God had forgiven him, but he asked for Corrie's forgiveness as well.

Corrie kept her hand at her side. How could she possibly forgive this man? She asked Jesus to help her forgive him, to give her his forgiveness since she had none of her own. As she explained what happened, "From my shoulder along my arm and through my hand a current seemed to pass from me to him, while into my heart sprang a love for this stranger that almost overwhelmed me. And so I discovered that it is not on our forgiveness any more than on our goodness that the world's healing hinges, but on His. When He tells us to love our enemies, He gives, along with the command, the love itself."

This is the crux of why you and I—petty, squabbling humans that we are—can transcend the limits of that humanness and offer forgiveness to

An Exercise in Forgiveness

If you are struggling, unable to forgive a person you regard as an enemy, try to pray for them instead of cursing them. Sit quietly where you won't be disturbed. Think of that individual and begin to focus God's love on them. You might imagine that love shining on them like a spotlight or warming them from the inside out. If your thoughts return to your anger at the person, quietly bring your focus back on God loving that person. This may be difficult at first. Remember that God's love is enough for everyone and that God offers forgiveness for all offenses.

Try to take some time like this every day to focus on the person whom you perceive as an enemy. "Be with this person, O God," you might pray. "Fill him with your love. Change his heart." You also might try to imagine what it is like to be that person. What is she struggling with? What hurts her heart? Sometimes when we "walk a mile in someone else's shoes," we find that our feet are not so different after all.

Write down any thoughts or feelings you have after these prayer times. You may begin to see your feelings alter toward the other person.

others. Don't we usually learn best by example? God has already given us the supreme example of forgiveness: God forgave those who crucified his Son, and through Jesus, God has forgiven you and me of all the things we do to hurt ourselves, others, or the world.

If we want to live as whole, healthy people, we must first reject the need to be right, to judge others, and to withhold forgiveness from those who have hurt us. In the next chapter we will look at why it's also important to forgive ourselves so that God can transform us. Meanwhile, Psalm 32:1 reminds us, "Happy are those whose transgression is forgiven, whose sin is covered."

Lord, make me an instrument of your peace,
  where there is hatred, let me sow love;
  where there is injury, pardon;
  where there is doubt, faith;
  where there is despair, hope;
  where there is darkness, light;
  where there is sadness, joy;
O Divine Master, grant that I may not so much seek
  to be consoled as to console;

⇀ Let Faith Help You Heal ↼

> **to be understood as to understand;**
> **to be loved as to love.**
> **For it is in giving that we receive;**
> **it is in pardoning that we are pardoned;**
> **and it is in dying that we are born to eternal life.**
>
> —Saint Francis of Assisi

Healing is not a one-shot deal. It is a journey and process by which we come to know ourselves better, understand and forgive other people, and grow closer to God. As you consider your own need and desire for healing, let your heart be guided by these words from Ephesians 4:31–32: "Put away from you all bitterness and wrath and anger and wrangling and slander, together with all malice, and be kind to one another, tenderhearted, forgiving one another, as God in Christ has forgiven you."

As you pray the following psalm, personalize it. Don't think of it as words written in ancient times. Instead, apply these words out of the fullness of your heart. And, after praying these words, you might want to write down your responses to these questions:

- What does this psalm say about God?
- What does this psalm say about me?
- When has God "redeemed my life from the Pit"?
- How in my life do I bless God's name?

Bless the Lord, O my soul, and all that is within me, bless his holy name. Bless the Lord, O my soul, and do not forget all his benefits—who forgives all your iniquity, who heals all your diseases, who redeems your life from the Pit, who crowns you with steadfast love and mercy, who satisfies you with good as long as you live so that your youth is renewed like the eagle's.

The Lord works vindication and justice for all who are oppressed. He made known his ways to Moses, his acts to the people of Israel. The Lord is merciful and gracious, slow to anger and abounding in steadfast love. He will not always accuse, nor will he keep his anger forever. He does not deal with us according to our sins, nor repay us according to our iniquities. For as the heavens are high above the earth, so great is his steadfast love toward those who fear him; as far as the east is from the west, so far he removes our transgressions from us. As a father has compassion for his children, so the Lord has compassion for those who fear him. For he knows how we were made; he remembers that we are dust.

As for mortals, their days are like grass; they flourish like a flower of the field; for the wind passes over it, and it is gone, and its place knows it no more. But the steadfast love of the Lord is from everlasting to everlasting on those who fear him, and his righteousness to children's children, to those who keep his covenant and remember to do his commandments.

The Lord has established his throne in the heavens, and his kingdom rules over all. Bless the Lord, O you his angels, you mighty ones who do his bidding, obedient to his spoken word. Bless the Lord, all his hosts, his ministers that do his will. Bless the Lord, all his works, in all places of his dominion. Bless the Lord, O my soul.

—Psalm 103

~~Let Faith Help You Heal~~

Forgive Yourself and Allow God to Transform Your Life

But now take another look. I'm going to give this city a thorough renovation, working a true healing inside and out. I'm going to show them life whole, life brimming with blessings.

Jeremiah 33:6 (The Message)

MARK'S FESTIVE Valentine's Day outing with his young son, Owen, was shattered when, distracted by Owen's high spirits, Mark ran a red light and plowed his van into an oncoming truck. Owen was killed instantly, and Mark spent a month in the hospital because of injuries sustained in the accident. The damage to his body healed over time, but Mark could not forgive himself for his son's death.

"What kind of father kills his own child?" he berated himself. His torment ate away at his relationship with his wife, Imelda. Depression clouded his view of everything about his life until one day Imelda sat him down and said, "I miss Owen, too. There's not a minute I don't think about him. But when I'm remembering him, I am *not* blaming you." She took his hand. "It was an accident, and unless you're able to forgive yourself for it, I will have lost both of you."

Mark and Imelda joined a local chapter of Compassionate Friends, a grief support group for parents whose children have died. Over time, Mark was able to forgive himself for his role in the accident and to think of Owen in joyful remembrance. Mark and Imelda did not have another child, but he volunteered to work with children in an after-school program. "I see other children who are the age Owen would have been, and I wonder what he would have been like," he said. "But I found meaning in my life once I forgave myself, which was probably the hardest thing I've ever done."

> *I need to get out of my own
> way if I am to heal.*
> Anne Wilson Schaef

As a young adult, Jacqueline loved to party. She didn't realize that her life was swinging out of control. Then, one night, she was arrested on a DUI. Shaken and humiliated, she cut back on her drinking and tried to straighten herself out. When she realized she was pregnant a few months later, Jacqueline chose to have the child even though she knew she was choosing a difficult path as a young, single mother.

"In some ways, that DUI was the best thing that could have happened to me," Jacqueline says now. "I think of it as God's wake-up call. Without the DUI, I might still have been heavily drinking and enjoying the nightlife when I discovered

I was pregnant. I might have made a different choice about the pregnancy."

By the time her daughter, Michelle, was born, Jacqueline had settled down, began attending a local church, and was able to be a responsible mother to the child. "Rather than focusing on my past behavior and the fact that I had an arrest on my record, I chose to forgive myself the mistakes I'd made. I refused to look at Michelle as a mistake. She's 13 now, and we're both active in our church. Michelle is growing up with the clear understanding that God loves her and will always forgive her. I hope she is also learning that there will be times when she needs to forgive herself."

For you, O Lord, are good and forgiving, abounding in steadfast love to all who call on you.

Psalm 86:5

Jesus understood how tricky forgiveness can be. Sometimes we think we've done something that cannot possibly be forgiven. Or if others condemn us, we may be convinced what we have done is unforgivable. We forget that God's love is enough to forgive even our worst acts. Again and again in the Bible, we see Jesus offering forgiveness to people: "Friend, your sins are forgiven." Remember the story of the woman caught in adultery who was brought before Jesus by the religious leaders? Imagine how she must have felt:

"Early in the morning he came again to the temple. All the people came to him and he sat down and began to teach them. The scribes and the Pharisees brought a woman who had been caught in adultery; and making her stand before all of them, they said to him, 'Teacher, this woman was caught in the very act of committing adultery. Now in the law Moses commanded us to stone such women. Now what do you say?' They said this to test him, so that they might have some charge to bring against him. Jesus bent down and wrote with his finger on the ground. When they kept on questioning him, he straightened up and said to them, 'Let anyone among you who is without sin be the first to throw a stone at her.' And once again he bent down and wrote on the ground. When they heard it, they went away, one by one, beginning with the elders; and Jesus was left alone with the woman standing before him. Jesus straightened up and said to her, 'Woman, where are they? Has no one condemned you?' She said, 'No one, sir.' And Jesus said, 'Neither do I condemn you. Go your way, and from now on do not sin again'" (John 8:2–11).

The scribes and the Pharisees were trying to get Jesus in trouble. By bringing an open-and-shut case of adultery (caught in the act!) they hoped to trap Jesus into violating religious law. Because Jesus associated with people they considered unworthy sinners, they expected him to turn the woman loose, thus breaking the law of Moses, whose words in Leviticus were clear: Adultery was to be punished by stoning. They hoped Jesus' own message of love and forgiveness would trip him up.

> *Forgiveness is not an occasional act, it is a permanent attitude.*
>
> Martin Luther King, Jr.

As so often happened in the Bible, Jesus did something surprising. He bent down to write in the dirt as the scribes and Pharisees questioned him about the case. When he stood up, he managed to confound the accusers, uphold the law of Moses, and set the woman free. "Let anyone among you who is without sin be the first to throw a stone at her," he said before returning to whatever he was writing on the ground.

What a dramatic moment! Everyone present was forced to look inward and acknowledge that none was without sin. You can bet that the woman, who was terrified she might be stoned to death, was doing some hard thinking and/or praying herself. "Has no one condemned you?" he asked, then uttered words that lead to new life for her: "Neither do I condemn you. Go your way, and from now on do not sin again."

Have you ever received such a gift of forgiveness? Were you able to accept the gift and go on with your life? Jesus did not condone what the woman did. He also understood the drama of what had just happened. Wouldn't any of us be changed if we thought we might die and yet received a reprieve?

If you forgive people enough, you belong to them, and they to you, whether either person likes it or not—squatters' rights of the heart.

James Hilton

Jesus offers the same forgiveness to all of us. Like Mark, Jacqueline, and the adulterous woman discovered, we must also forgive ourselves if we are to grasp the gift of forgiveness from others. "Forgive us our sins as we forgive those who sin against us" we say in the Lord's Prayer, and we must take it one step further: "Help us forgive ourselves as we forgive others."

Since Bill Wilson founded Alcoholics Anonymous in 1935, countless individuals have turned away from dependency on alcohol and transformed their lives. Of the 12 steps AA members take in their process toward wholeness, steps four through ten are the most explicitly related to asking for and receiving forgiveness. Read these steps (which are useful even if you aren't struggling with addiction issues), and consider whether working through these steps in your own life might be a crucial step toward your search for wholeness and healing. What would it be like if we:

─ LET FAITH HELP YOU HEAL ─

4. Made a searching and fearless moral inventory of ourselves.
5. Admitted to God, to ourselves, and to another human being the exact nature of our wrongs.
6. Were entirely ready to have God remove all these defects of character.
7. Humbly asked Him to remove our shortcomings.
8. Made a list of all persons we had harmed, and became willing to make amends to them all.
9. Made direct amends to such people wherever possible, except when to do so would injure them or others.
10. Continued to take personal inventory, and when we were wrong, promptly admitted it.

Did any of these steps jump out at you? Is there some issue you want to work on? True healing, whether physical, emotional, or spiritual, is most likely to occur when you have forgiven yourself and others and are ready to move forward into healing and wholeness.

The refusal to forgive and be forgiven lies at the root of a great deal of sickness. Like a root it is often as not hidden. For true health we have to forgive God, others, and ourselves.

Philip Pare

Some of us have committed extremely hurtful sins for which we need forgiveness. Others of us are guilty of the usual garden variety of human failings: jealousy, bitterness, lying, and pettiness. Yet no matter how seemingly small the sin, each of us knows that we have displeased God and hurt ourselves and others in some way. Whether we rage against a loved one, twist the truth to make ourselves look better, or wish we had a bigger house or newer car, all of us have failed to live according to God's high standard of righteousness.

Let Faith Help You Heal

J. Neville Ward wrote, "There is so much for us all to forgive that we shall never get it done without putting in a lot of practice." As we move toward wholeness and healing, we must put forgiveness of others and ourselves in daily practice.

*Come, my Light, and illumine
my darkness.
Come, my Life, and revive me from death.
Come, my Physician, and heal my wounds.
Come, Flame of divine love, and burn up
the thorns of my sins,
Kindling my heart with
the flame of thy love.
Come, my King, sit upon the throne
of my heart and reign there.
For thou alone art my King
and my Lord. Amen.*

Dimitri of Rostov

Are there things you have not yet let go of? Have you withheld forgiveness from yourself? Is there anything from your past that might prevent you from healing? Take a few minutes to consider your life. You could write down things for which you still crave forgiveness. Or you could say them out loud. Perhaps you need to talk to a friend, minister, counselor, or family member about a past situation.

Come home, come home;
You who are weary, come home;
Earnestly, tenderly, Jesus is calling,
Calling, O sinner, come home!

Will L. Thompson

If you are serious about letting your faith help you heal, now is the time to say with the psalmist, "O Lord my God, I cried to you for help, and you have healed me " (Psalm 30:2) or "This is my comfort in my distress, that your promise gives me life" (Psalm 119:50). Trust God to love you no matter what, to accept you, sins and all, and to offer forgiveness that leads to healing.

A compost pile starts out as a mess of banana peels, tea bags, melon rinds, grass clippings, and other organic material. These materials (considered "waste" by many people) decompose into rich earth that rivals any store-bought fertilizer. Marjorie Thompson wrote, "Our life experience is not unlike compost. If we allow it to be aerated by grace, if we are patient with the conditions of each day, in time it will become the rich soil of new life. God is always working for good for those who love God."

So if you think there are parts of your life you aren't proud of, things you've done that you wish you hadn't, consider it all compost—material that has made you who you are, leading you to the present but which doesn't have to hold you back from a healed and whole future.

↦ Let Faith Help You Heal ↤

> *Of one thing I am certain,
> the body is not the measure of
> healing, peace is the measure.*
>
> Phyllis McGinley

In chapter two, you came up with a Healing Vision Statement. Turn to page 39 to review that statement. Are you ready to accept transformation in your life? Remember Bartimaeus, who followed Jesus after he was healed? Or the man by the Sheep Gate pool who had to give up dependency on others and literally stand on his own two feet? The woman caught in adultery was told to sin no more; we assume she didn't go back to the man with whom she was caught. With the wholeness offered to these people came change and transformation.

**Lord,
I like the part about "new" and "better,"
but what's that going to look like? Feel like?
What's all this going to mean?
I want transformation,**

←Let Faith Help You Heal→

> But the change part scares me.
> Give me strength, Lord.
> Help me accept your gift of new life.
> Lead me forward.
> I put my trust in you.
> Amen.

Change can be hard. A new job could necessitate a move across the country. Good health might mean we have to give up the attentive sympathy from people who feel sorry for our ailments. Turning from certain negative habits might call for changing our friendship network.

What is your history of change? You might want to draw out a horizontal timeline of your life from birth until the present, marking times you experienced great change, such as starting school, moving to a new house, deaths of significant people, and other important transitions. Put a check mark by those times when you were able to comfortably weather the change and an asterisk by the times when that change was difficult for you. Which of these categories do you fit into?

I Liked Things the Way They Were: You resist change whenever possible and take a long time to feel comfortable in a new situation.

Just Give Me Time to Adjust: Although you are initially uncomfortable, you know that given time, you'll be fine with any change.

I Can Do This: You go into a new situation with a positive attitude and have figured out ways to make the transition as easy as possible.

Change? What Change?: You easily jump from one situation to another with no need for transition.

Jesus offers you healing and new life. What do you have to give up in order to accept this gift? Do you have to adjust your attitude about the familiarity of the known when you experience a change in your circumstances? The caterpillar may feel quite content with its earth-born life, but it was meant to change into a butterfly and take to the skies. God wants us to live full, positive lives.

Let Faith Help You Heal

For the love of God is broader than the measure of our mind;
And the heart of the Eternal is most wonderfully kind.

Frederick W. Faber

"I was a third-generation welfare recipient," says Lucille. "I was determined to get out of the projects to give my children a better future, so I stayed in school even though I was a teenage mother. I went to night school and finished college, even though it took me seven years. I don't regret any of it, but it was hard."

Lucille credits her church congregation with giving her the spiritual and emotional support that kept her going. "I knew a core group of people were praying for me, and when I got down, that lifted me up."

Along with the positive changes were some surprises, as well. "I had to fight some people's negative expectations of me. They knew my history and thought I'd end up like my mother and grandmother. Then there was the opposite reaction after I was in my first home and working for the Post Office. So much was expected of me! It made me a little crazy for awhile, being caught between the people who thought I couldn't do it, and the people who thought I could do anything."

O gracious and holy Father,
Give us wisdom to perceive you,
intelligence to understand you,
diligence to seek you,
patience to wait for you,
eyes to see you,
a heart to meditate on you,
and a life to proclaim you,
through the power of the spirit of
    Jesus Christ our Lord.

—Saint Benedict

Whatever your response to change in your life, remember that God has great plans for you.

"Do not remember the former things, or consider the things of old. I am about to do a new thing; now it springs forth, do you not perceive it?" (Isaiah 43:18–19). You will not be alone as you experience transformation. The newness—a gift of healing, wholeness, and new life—will be a gift from the good God who loves you. All you have to do is forgive yourself and open your hands and heart to receive the new life God wants to give you.

Let Go of That Which Binds You

If there be anywhere on earth [where] a lover of God is always kept safe from falling, I know nothing of it, for it was not shown me. But this was shown: that in falling and rising again we are always kept in the same precious love.

Julian of Norwich

As VICE PRESIDENT of an advertising agency and active in the community, LaKeesha continually strived for achievement. The agency's CEO said, "LaKeesha is always at the top of her game." Those closest to her, however, had a different take on her drivenness: "She's obsessed with success."

When a coworker shouted, "You don't care who you step on as you fight your way to the top, do you?" LaKeesha took a hard look at her need to achieve. She realized that the rush she got from meeting goals went beyond healthy achievement and professionalism. "I couldn't control my need to be the best. As soon as I received accolades on a project, I took off to chase the next objective. I could never rest, not for a minute."

LaKeesha went into therapy to seriously examine her compulsion to be the best no matter what the consequences. Over time, she realized that her addiction to overachieve could be addressed only at a spiritual level. "I had to realize that in God's eyes, I was enough whether I got a big contract or not, whether others applauded me or not. I had to let go of my need for the approval of my colleagues and the agency CEO."

As with many addicts, through counseling, LaKeesha discovered that she had suffered a childhood trauma she had repressed for 24 years. Her childhood pain had manifested itself years later in her need to prove herself and to build walls between herself and other people.

Let Faith Help You Heal

"I needed to be healed of that past abuse so I could move on and become healthy again," LaKeesha said.

Addictions come in many forms. A person can be addicted to alcohol, work, food, drugs, shopping, gambling, sex, tobacco, pornography, or anything that gives a pleasurable "high." When someone is dependent on a particular practice and can't control that dependency, it is an addiction.

All addictions lead to the spiritual, emotional, physical, and social destruction of the addict.

Stephen Earll

The Random House Dictionary defines "addiction" as "the state of being enslaved to a habit or practice or to something that is psychologically or physically habit-forming, as narcotics, to such an extent that its cessation causes severe trauma." Psychiatrist Gerald May identified 105 things to which people can become attached to the point of addiction. Some are positive things (exercise, food, work) when not abused to the point of addiction. Others (drugs, alcohol, pornography, tobacco) can be dangerous even when used in moderation.

All of these addictive tendencies have in common their affect on the addictive personality. A healthy person can go shop for items when necessary. Someone who is addicted to shopping can't think of anything else. A healthy person likes a drink once in a while. An alcoholic finds he or she needs more and more drinks to maintain the same "buzz" that used to come with one or two drinks. The addicted person denies their dependency on tobacco or heroin or sex and cannot keep in perspective the possible destructiveness of her or his behavior.

There are many reasons a person clings to his or her addictions. Perhaps that extra line of cocaine helps a woman forget how lonely she is. Or the addiction to work makes a man feel powerful. By engaging in random, indiscriminate sex, a man doesn't have to face his mortality and the fact that he's the same age his father was when he died.

Whatever reason the addicted person started down that path, Gerald May would say, "Spiritually, addiction is a deep-seated form of idolatry. The objects of our addictions become our false gods. These are what we worship, what we attend to, where we give our time and energy, instead of love. Addiction, then, displaces and supplants God's love as the source and object of our deepest true desire."

Saint Augustine wrote, "Our hearts are restless until they rest in you [God]." All addictions, no matter what the initial reasons for addictive behavior, reflect this restlessness, this need for connection with the Almighty. This is why Alcoholics Anonymous and other 12-step programs begin: "We admitted we were powerless over alcohol—that our lives had become unmanageable" and follow with two important steps. We...

2. Came to believe that a Power greater than ourselves could restore us to sanity.
3. Made a decision to turn our will and our lives over to the care of God as we understand God.

Most of the 12 steps are infused with this spiritual sense that healing (from addictions or other diseases and conditions) comes through faith in God as well as the individual's own hard work.

O Love of God, descend into my heart;
Enlighten the dark corners of this neglected dwelling,
And scatter there Your cheerful beams.
Dwell in the soul that longs to be Your temple;
Water that barren soil overrun with weeds and briars
And lost for lack of cultivating.
Make it fruitful with Your dew.
Come, dear Refreshment of those who languish;
Come, Star and Guide of those who
    sail amidst tempests.
You are the Haven of the tossed and shipwrecked.
Come now, Glory and Crown of the living,
As well as the Safeguard of the dying.
Come, Sacred Spirit;
Come, and make me fit to receive You.

—Saint Augustine

Let Faith Help You Heal

Jesus often healed people who were, in the words of his time, "possessed by demons." People today might describe it differently: "When my body shakes and I am desperate for the next fix, I don't feel like myself" or "It's almost as though I'm possessed by the addiction at times. I don't feel I have any control over what I do." As you read the dramatic story below, think what life was like for a man who had to be guarded and chained to protect him from whatever demons drove his destructive behavior.

"Then they arrived at the country of the Gerasenes, which is opposite Galilee. As he stepped out on land, a man of the city who had demons met him. For a long time he had worn no clothes, and he did not live in a house but in the tombs. When he saw Jesus, he fell down before him and shouted at the top of his voice, 'What have you to do with me, Jesus, Son of the Most High God? I beg you, do not torment me'—for Jesus had commanded the unclean spirit to come out of the man. (For many times it had seized him; he was kept under guard and bound with chains and shackles, but he would break the bonds and be driven by the demon into the wilds.) Jesus then asked him, 'What is your name?' He said, 'Legion'; for many demons had entered him. They begged him not to order them to go back into the abyss.

"Now there on the hillside a large herd of swine was feeding; and the demons begged Jesus to let them enter these. So he gave them permission. Then the demons came out of the man and entered the swine, and the herd rushed down the steep bank into the lake and was drowned.

"When the swineherds saw what had happened, they ran off and told it in the city and in the country. Then people came out to see what had happened, and when they came to Jesus, they found the man from whom the demons had gone sitting at the feet of Jesus, clothed and in his right mind. And they were afraid. Those who had seen it told them how the one who had been possessed by demons had been healed. Then all the people of the surrounding country of the Gerasenes asked Jesus to leave them; for they were seized with great fear. So he got into the boat and returned. The man from whom the demons had gone begged that he might be with him; but Jesus sent him away, saying, 'Return to your home, and declare how much God has done for you.' So he went away, proclaiming throughout the city how much Jesus had done for him" (Luke 8:26–39).

Notice that Jesus asked the man, "What is your name?" Jesus is always personal. He wants to know us and love us as we are. In this case, when Jesus sent the demons out of the man, the man wanted to stay by Jesus' side, but Jesus sent the healed man off to share the good news of God's power.

This story is about more than demons, pigs, and swineherds. Jesus literally freed a man who was formerly bound and chained. We don't need to know how and why the man was in such a state.

Let Faith Help You Heal

What matters is that Jesus set the man free from what he had been and what bound him. John Townroe says, "Inner healing is concerned to bring to light the causes of the inner pain: to help the sufferer to interpret them correctly; and to release the person from the emotional grip of the past."

Come to me, all you that are weary and are carrying heavy burdens, and I will give you rest.

Matthew 11:28

Some people may experience instantaneous healing from addictions. In most cases, however, after realizing that help is needed and calling on God for sustenance, addicted persons need outside help to conquer the addiction. Some people will find success in therapeutic counseling. Others do best with a detox and/or rehab program, and they may need a lifetime of attendance at such support groups as Alcoholics or Gamblers Anonymous.

Let Faith Help You Heal

Each person must find what works to help him or her overcome addictions. If you're struggling to let go of something that binds you, use whatever methods, tools, and resources are necessary for you to move away from addictive behaviors and toward God's wholeness in your life. Like the man possessed with demons, you can look forward to casting off the chains that bind you. Think of what life free from addictions could look like. Are you ready for that transformation?

Organizations that might help you overcome an addiction:

- Alcoholics Anonymous (www.alcoholics-anonymous.org)
- Overeaters Anonymous (www.oa.org)
- Narcotics Anonymous (www.na.org)
- Co-Dependents Anonymous (http://codependents.org/)
- Sex Addicts Anonymous (http://saa-recovery.org)

— Let Faith Help You Heal —

- Gamblers Anonymous (www.gamblersanonymous.org)

No matter which methods and resources you use as you work to change addictive behaviors, these suggestions may also prove useful:

- Find ways to connect with God every day.
- Take time to know yourself.
- Acknowledge your needs.
- Get professional help.
- Surround yourself with supportive, nurturing people.
- Choose to be happy and whole.
- Be gentle with yourself.
- Enter fully into the process of overcoming your addiction.
- Replace the addiction with a positive behavior.
- Believe new life is possible.
- Remember: God made you; God loves you; God wants the best for you.
- Let go of previous expectations of yourself.

- Give yourself permission to try new behaviors.
- Stay grounded spiritually.
- Trust the professionals who encourage and challenge you.

You might want to choose one of these statements to write on an index card to use as a repeated prayer. "I choose to be happy and whole." "God made me; God loves me; God wants the best for me." "I will be gentle with myself."

He did not say, "You will never have a rough passage, you will never be overstrained, you will never feel uncomfortable," but he did say, "You will never be overcome."

Julian of Norwich

What is it that binds you and prevents you from health and wholeness? Addictions plague some people, but other people struggle with past abuses or broken relationships that hold them back. Just as the addict must shed behaviors that impede growth and imprison them, so people who are not addicted may have past traumas of which they need to be free.

Georgia lurched from one bad relationship to another and found herself finalizing her third divorce at 41, once again lonely, sad, and feeling abandoned. "I can't figure out what is wrong with me," she told a counselor. "I wasn't abused as a child. I had a great mother and managed without my father. Yet I seem to get into relationships where I'm always trying to please the man at my own expense."

Therapy helped Georgia see how she responded to the world out of her feeling of abandonment because her father had left the family when she was five. Unable to articulate her feelings of loss and responsibility, the young Georgia had thrown herself into the search for a father figure who could help her feel safe and secure again. "I finally realized—duh!—that my expectations of every relationship were unrealistic. I needed to claim my own strength and let go of my need to please the father I hadn't seen since I was a little girl. I'm still a work in progress, but I want to be healthy and whole. I want to enter a relationship out of my strength and not out of my little girl lostness."

Inner healing is simply this: Jesus can take the memories of our past and heal them... and fill with his love all these places in us that have been empty for so long, once they have been healed and drained of the poison of past hates and resentment.

Francis MacNutt

Perhaps you have moments in life where you feel disconnected, lost, or confused. You may not remember a specific event in your past that brought you to your present feelings. You may not understand why your relationships have not felt healthy or why you just feel "stuck." Is there something binding you of which you need to let go? Are you ready to take hold of a new freedom in your life?

Try this guided meditation, which is based on Psalm 139 (The Message). It may work best if you either have a trusted friend read it to you, or you can tape-record the words ahead of time and listen to them in private. (Whichever way you choose, the reader should pause for at least 30 seconds whenever there are asterisks in the meditation. This leaves time for your mind to visualize what the words suggest.) Begin by finding a place and time where you will not be disturbed or distracted. Sit comfortably without crossing your legs or arms. Close your eyes. Take several deep breaths, and try to center yourself and focus your mind. As you hear the words of the meditation, let images play out in your mind like your own private movie screen. There are no right or wrong images; just let yourself relax into the images. When you have completed the meditation, you may want to journal about the experience or draw any images that came to you.

> Imagine that you are walking on a beach by yourself when you hear a comforting voice calling your name. ***
>
> The voice says, "I shaped you first inside, then out; I formed you in your mother's womb. ***
>
> I know you inside and out, every bone in your body. I know exactly how you were made, bit by bit, how you were sculpted from nothing into something. ***
>
> Like an open book, I watched you grow from conception to birth; all the stages of your life were spread out before me, and I have loved you every moment of your life. ***
>
> When other people hurt you, I felt that hurt deeply. ***
>
> When you made choices that were not in your best interest, I stayed by your side. ***
>
> I have cried when you cried, and laughed when you laughed. Your joy has been my joy, and your sorrows have cut me to the quick. I

know even the wounds you have not admitted to yourself. ***

Do you want to be healed? You have but to ask. Seek, and you shall find. Ask, and it shall be given unto you. ***

I offer you wholeness, my child. I want to remake you as I made you in your beginning. How do you need to be remade? What is it you need to be whole?" ***

The voice fades, but you stand on the beach, feeling the heat of the sand and sun. Which of God's words reverberates inside you? ***

Thank God for all of God's gifts, including the opportunity to begin again. When you are ready, open your eyes and return to the present moment.

It is time to let go of whatever is holding you in bondage—of whatever is preventing you from living as the whole, healthy person God created. Do you want to be healed? Healing may not happen overnight, but you can trust God to be with you as you embark on this journey. And, as Tori Amos said, "Healing takes courage, and we all have courage, even if we have to dig a little to find it." Knowing you are not alone but are sustained by God should give you extra courage for whatever work you need to do in order to achieve healing.

As you embark on this exciting and possibly terrifying journey, keep the following prayer by Reinhold Neibuhr before you:

God give us grace to accept with serenity the things that cannot be changed, courage to change the things that should be changed, and wisdom to distinguish the one from the other.

—Let Faith Help You Heal—

Realize That You Are a Wounded Healer

The only work that will ultimately bring any good to any of us is the work of contributing to the healing of the world.

Marianne Williamson

When she was 17, a diving accident left Joni Earekson paralyzed from the neck down. Instead of going off to college as the active young woman she had been, Joni spent two rough years in rehabilitation. How could she live without the use of her hands? What would her life be like? Joni struggled with depression and suicidal tendencies until she prayed, "God, if I can't die, then please show me how to live. 'Cos I can't do this thing called 'paralysis.' I can't, I can't do this. I have no strength for this. But you do and I need you big time."

Joni not only worked on physical rehabilitation, adjusting to the reality that the rest of her life would be spent in a wheelchair, but she focused on spiritual growth as well. Once she realized that God could use her even in this altered state, Joni began the next fruitful stage of a remarkable life. She taught herself to paint with a brush between her teeth and became an accomplished artist, and she wrote her autobiography, *Joni*.

Over the next 30 years, Joni established herself as an artist, author, conference speaker, actress, and disability advocate. She founded Joni and Friends, a Christian ministry to and about the disability community. She has used her own experience to inspire people with disabilities to live a full life and to raise awareness of disability issues in society.

Healing yourself is connected with healing others.

Yoko Ono

Let Faith Help You Heal

When we see a quadriplegic or a burn-scarred person, we can guess that they have undergone periods of healing and that the experience probably changed them. Other people carry their wounds inside. We all carry wounds, whether visible or invisible. We often feel the need to hide those wounds, to look strong and unbeatable, but as Joni's example reminds us, that which wounded us can also be a gift to others. Even if we haven't completely healed from whatever needs healing, we can reach out to others and share who and what we are.

Henri J. M. Nouwen expanded on the Jungian concept of the "wounded healer" by saying, "For a deep understanding of his own pain makes it possible for him to convert his weakness into strength and to offer his own experience as a source of healing to those who are often lost in the darkness of their own misunderstood sufferings."

In other words, our own particular pain and history can be part of our gift to the world. That's part of the reason 12-step groups are so successful. Individuals attending those groups are in various stages of sobriety and change. They know how difficult it can be to give up particular addictions. They support each other out of that mutual understanding. Cancer survivors, grieving parents, those recovering from sexual abuse or unhealthy relationships all fill a particular need in the lives of others in similar situations.

The I in illness is isolation, and the crucial letters in wellness are we.

Author unknown

"The first time I was invited to facilitate a breast cancer survivors' group, I was terrified," Marlene remembers. "I wasn't an expert on cancer. I only knew my own experience, which had not been positive. It turned out that my experience was enough. I could relate to the fear, anger, grief—all the feelings a diagnosis of breast cancer can bring up. I've led groups now for seven years."

Throughout history, "tender loving care" has uniformly been recognized as a valuable element in healing.

Larry Dossey

King David knew grief. Because he took Uriah's wife, Bathsheba, arranged for Uriah to be killed, and had a child with Bathsheba, David suffered the consequences. "The Lord struck the child that Uriah's wife bore to David, and it became very ill. David therefore pleaded with God for the child; David fasted, and went in and lay all night on the ground. The elders of his house stood beside him, urging him to rise from the ground; but he would not, nor did he eat food with them" (2 Samuel 12:15–17).

Out of that grief came some of the most poignant writings about life, love, death, and loss. The psalms cover all the emotional bases; David understood both the highs and lows of life. The psalmist reminds us how after God heals us, we can participate in another's healing:

Dignify those who are down on their luck; you'll feel good—
 that's what God does.
God looks after us all,
 makes us robust with life—
Lucky to be in the land,
 we're free from enemy worries.
Whenever we're sick and in bed,
 God becomes our nurse,
 nurses us back to health.

—Psalm 41:3 (The Message)

While Jesus suffered on the cross, he looked down and saw a group of his followers, including his grieving mother and one of his closest disciples. He understood the pain they each felt at his dying and how they could help each other out of their unique or shared experiences.

"Meanwhile, standing near the cross of Jesus were his mother, and his mother's sister, Mary the wife of Clopas, and Mary Magdalene. When Jesus saw his mother and the disciple whom he loved standing beside her, he said to his mother, 'Woman, here is your son.' Then he said to the disciple, 'Here is your mother.' And from that hour the disciple took her into his own home" (John 19:25–27).

Soon after he made the connection between his mother and friend, Jesus died. Although he was no longer present in body, he had ensured that they did not have to grieve alone.

The friend who can be silent with us in a moment of despair or confusion, who can stay with us in an hour of grief and bereavement, who can tolerate not knowing...not healing, not curing...that is a friend who cares.

Henri J. M. Nouwen

When Paul's young wife died, he took a leave from his job and cut himself off from their network of friends. Day after day, Paul stayed inside his home, curtains drawn, and wondered why he had been left alone. One day the doorbell rang, and when Paul didn't answer it, he heard the voice of his accountant, Eugene:

"I know you're home, Paul. Please let me in."

Paul sat on the couch and made no movement toward the door.

"I'm going to stand here 'til you open the door."

Paul sank back against the couch pillows.

"And it's cold out here," Eugene yelled.

After 15 minutes of this running commentary, Paul let Eugene into the house, but he didn't say a word. The accountant sat next to his client on the couch. He didn't say anything either until half an hour had passed.

"I'll come to your house every day after I get off work at five," Eugene said gently. "We don't have to talk, Paul, but I don't want you to sit here all alone."

Eugene left, came back the next day, and kept his promise. Each day, Paul let him in. They sat on the couch in silence until a week later when Paul spoke.

"This means a lot," he said, and that was the end of the conversation.

Little by little, Paul opened up. He didn't talk about Linda's death or his grief or why he had become reclusive. Eugene didn't pry or push. After nine weeks, Paul was ready to reenter the world of work and friends. He later said, "I'm not sure I would have survived without Eugene. He wasn't the only one who reached out to me, but he was the most persistent. I'd been so focused on life without Linda, I'd forgotten that other people also cared."

Eugene was able to reach out to Paul because he had experienced deep grief; his twin sister had died of leukemia when he was in college. He remembered the pain, the emptiness, and how hard it was to connect with other people who hadn't understood his grief. Eugene was the wounded healer who brought Paul back to life.

I'm touched by the idea that when we do things that are useful and helpful—collecting these shards of spirituality—that we may be helping to bring about a healing.

Leonard Nimoy

What wounds have you endured that might prompt you to help another person? Is there a way your healing process can be shared with someone who may be at a different stage in their own healing? Fill out the following questionnaire to see how you might make a difference:

My Life Experience (check all that apply and add other experiences that might help you be a wounded healer at the bottom of the list):

Let Faith Help You Heal

___ I have lost a loved one.
___ I have experienced life-threatening illness.
___ I have suffered sexual abuse.
___ I once thought of killing myself.
___ I am a cancer survivor.
___ I have been hurt in a love relationship.
___ I have suffered mental illness.
___ I have fought addictions.
___ I live with a disability.
___ I have been depressed.
___ I have had money problems.
___ I experienced physical abuse.
___ I have felt alone and without friends.
___ _____
___ _____
___ _____

Most of us will check one or more statements on the above list. As Anatole France said, "The truth is that life is delicious, horrible, charming, frightful, sweet, bitter, and that is everything." We may live healthy, happy, fulfilled lives, but that doesn't mean we will never experience death, illness, times of despair, and sadness. As wounded healers, we can use those experiences to help others through similar times.

Making one's own wounds a source of healing, therefore, does not call for a sharing of superficial personal pains but for a constant willingness to see one's own pain and suffering as rising from the depth of the human condition which all [people] share.

Henri J. M. Nouwen

Look at your list and ask yourself, "Who can I help?" You may know someone who is going through what you experienced. You may decide to volunteer with an organization that offers help to a specific group of individuals. Or you may just remain open to the possibility of meeting someone who might inspire you to action. Whatever pain and trauma you may have experienced can strengthen you and help you be a "wounded healer" for others.

As a child, Jean Vanier escaped Nazi Europe on a refugee boat from France. At the end of World War II, he met Holocaust survivors and was affected by their suffering. Later, he served in England's Royal Navy and the Royal Canadian Navy before receiving a doctorate in philosophy. When he became aware of the horrible conditions under which many people with developmental disabilities lived, he invited two institutionalized men to live with him in his home, "L'Arche."

Vanier explained: "What I discover today is every time I see a man or a woman with a severe mental handicap—the incredible cry that is coming from them—what I would call the primal cry—which is, 'Do you love me?'—a very deep cry. And you find with people with mental handicaps that this is their—'Do you love me?,' 'Why have I been abandoned?,' or 'Has my life any value?'"

Young people from around the world were intrigued with Vanier's concept of living in community with people who had formerly been discounted and locked away. Eventually, 104 other communities were founded in more than 30 countries on five continents. The ministry of L'Arche is not a one-way, "let's help these unfortunate people" concept. Those who came to L'Arche as assistants realized that everyone in the community contributed, whether they were developmentally disabled or not. Disabled persons are paired with those without a handicap to live and work together.

Some might have looked at the developmentally disabled people as wounded, not whole. Yet they were able to minister to others simply by being themselves and living out of their experience. Vanier says, "I have learned more about the Gospels from handicapped people, those on the margins of our society, those who have been crushed and hurt, than I have from the wise and prudent. Through their own growth and acceptance and surrender, wounded people have taught me that I must learn to accept my weakness and not pretend to be strong and capable. Handicapped people have shown me how handicapped I am, how handicapped we all are. They have reminded me that we are all weak and all called to death and that these are the realities of which we are most afraid."

**There is a light in this world,
a healing spirit
more powerful than any darkness we may encounter.
We sometimes lose sight of this force
when there is suffering, and too much pain.
Then suddenly,
the spirit will emerge
through the lives of ordinary people who hear a call
and answer in extraordinary ways.**

—Mother Teresa

The New Testament's epistles are filled with reminders that God's people are to help and support each other through thick and thin:

"And we urge you, beloved, to admonish the idlers, encourage the fainthearted, help the weak, be patient with all of them" (1 Thessalonians 5:14).

"As God's chosen ones, holy and beloved, clothe yourselves with compassion, kindness, humility, meekness, and patience. Bear with one another and, if anyone has a complaint against another, forgive each other; just as the Lord has forgiven you, so you also must forgive. Above all, clothe yourselves with love, which binds everything together in perfect harmony. And let the peace of Christ rule in your hearts, to which indeed you were called in the one body. And be thankful. Let the word of Christ dwell in you richly; teach and admonish one another in all wisdom; and with gratitude in your hearts sing psalms, hymns, and spiritual songs to God. And whatever you do, in word or deed, do everything in the name of the Lord Jesus, giving thanks to God the Father through him" (Colossians 3:12–17).

"Are any among you suffering? They should pray. Are any cheerful? They should sing songs of praise. Are any among you sick? They should call for the elders of the church and have them pray over them, anointing them with oil in the name of the Lord. The prayer of faith will save the sick, and the Lord will raise them up; and anyone who has committed sins will be forgiven. Therefore confess your sins to one another, and pray for one another, so that you may be healed. The prayer of the righteous is powerful and effective" (James 5:13–16).

> I have resolved to pray more and pray always, to pray in all places where quietness inviteth: in the house, on the highway and on the street; and to know no street or passage in this city that may not witness that I have not forgotten God.
>
> I purpose to take occasion of praying upon the sight of any church which I may pass, that God may be worshipped there in spirit, and that souls may be saved there;
>
> to pray for my sick patients and for the patients of other physicians;

> at my entrance into any home to say,... May the peace of God abide here;
>
> after hearing a sermon, to pray for a blessing on God's truth, and upon the messenger;
>
> upon the sight of a beautiful person to bless God for His creatures, to pray for the beauty of such one's soul, that God may enrich her with inward graces, and that the outward and inward may correspond;
>
> upon the sight of a deformed person, to pray to God to give them wholeness of soul, and by and by to give them the beauty of the resurrection.
>
> —Sir Thomas Browne, 1605

All of your experiences, positive and negative, have formed you into the person you are today. Whether you have only recently acknowledged your need for healing or have been actively working on the healing process for some time, your healing can be enriched by joining with others on their journeys. We need other people's support, wisdom, experience, and love. As wounded healers, we can turn even the most painful periods of our lives into fertile earth from which the seeds of healing can grow. "By his wounds you have been healed," Peter said (1 Peter 2:24). The Lord who himself endured and understood human suffering will be with us as we continue our own healing and walk beside others on their way to healing.

Thank you, Lord, for enduring unimaginable pain, even to the point of death, so that my broken relationship with my heavenly Father can be healed. By that healing, may all my emotional wounds be healed as well.

In your name, I pray. Amen.

Thank God for Your New Life

As we express our gratitude, we must never forget that the highest appreciation is not to utter words, but to live by them.

John F. Kennedy

W E'VE LOOKED AT different ways people need healing and some of the ways in which healing happens. You may have a new understanding of what healing is, how your faith can heal you, and how your own life can change in a positive way. Hopefully, you have begun your own healing process.

So what happens after healing? This story from Luke 17:11–19 gives us important clues:

"On the way to Jerusalem Jesus was going through the region between Samaria and Galilee. As he entered a village, ten lepers approached him. Keeping their distance, they called out, saying, 'Jesus, Master, have mercy on us!' When he saw them, he said to them, 'Go and show yourselves to the priests.' And as they went, they were made clean. Then one of them, when he saw that he was healed, turned back, praising God with a loud voice. He prostrated himself at Jesus' feet and thanked him. And he was a Samaritan. Then Jesus asked, 'Were not ten made clean? But the other nine, where are they? Was none of them found to return and give praise to God except this foreigner?' Then he said to him, 'Get up and go on your way; your faith has made you well.'"

Ten asked for and received healing. Ten ran to show the priests they were well. But only one turned back, praised God, and gave thanks to Jesus.

This story focuses not on the healing miracle itself but on the appropriate response to healing. Let's take a closer look at what happened to these ten lepers. First, we should remember that leprosy in the time of Jesus was more than a skin disease.

Lepers were not allowed to live with other people, even their own families. Lepers were social pariahs who were not allowed to worship in the temple. Many people assumed that a leper's disease was the result of the leper's own sin or the sins of others in the family. The ostracized leper might as well have been walking around with a huge **L** across their forehead. **L** for Leper, Loser, and Leave Me Alone.

Notice that the first thing Jesus did was to send the lepers to the local priest, who had the power to declare someone unclean or clean. It was only after the lepers turned away from Jesus that they were healed. They trusted him enough to follow his directions even before they saw physical changes in their bodies. They knew that only the priest could declare them fit to be part of society again, and surely they were desperate to belong to the community again.

Realizing that he had been made well, one man turned back to Jesus. The Greek word for his response comes from the same root as Doxology. The Samaritan leper praised God from whom his blessings—and healing—flowed. Jesus then questioned him about the other nine ("Were not ten made clean? Where are they?") and said, "Get up. On your way. Your faith has healed and saved you" (The Message).

But, wait! The leper was already healed of his disease. This implies that while the first healing was of his physical condition, the second healing was of a spiritual nature. The other nine lepers trusted Jesus and followed his instructions. The tenth, as anxious as he must have been to get the "all clear" from the priest so he could return to his family as a healed man, was thankful enough to stop, praise God, and thank Jesus for the gift of healing.

Saying thank you is more than good manners. It is good spirituality.

Alfred Painter

When colon cancer invaded his body, Carlos received a colostomy. "You can be thankful we caught it when we did," his surgeon said.

Yeah, right, thought Carlos, who resented the changes an ostomy pouch added to his lifestyle. Every time he emptied his pouch Carlos felt a twinge of resentment. *Why me? Why this stupid pouch?*

While Carlos was undergoing his colostomy, another surgeon performed an identical operation on 17-year-old Audrey, whose mother set the tone for the daughter's attitude.

"You are alive, Audrey. Never discount that fact. Because of this surgery, you can live a long and healthy life."

Audrey's mother signed her up for an ostomy support group, where the young woman found many others who managed the physical and emotional aspects of living after colostomies.

"Some of the others in my group have dealt with ostomy pouches for 30 years," Audrey often tells people, "and the technology of managing a colostomy is so much better now than it was when they had their surgery. I trust that the doctors and hospitals will find new ways to improve the procedures. Until then, dealing with the bag is a small price to pay for getting to hang out with my friends, finish high school, and look forward to college."

Despite the occasional difficult moments in Audrey's life ("Can I find a boyfriend who isn't grossed out by my bag?"), she is able to put things in perspective ("If I'd died of cancer, I would never have had a boyfriend."). Perhaps Carlos will one day meet someone like Audrey and catch hold of her positive attitude. Who knows? The other nine lepers, once they'd rushed to the priest for his appraisal, might eventually have remembered to give thanks for their healing.

LET FAITH HELP YOU HEAL

The hardest arithmetic to master is that which enables us to count our blessings.

Eric Hoffer

The Bible is filled with reminders that we are to thank God for everything in our lives:

I will give thanks to the Lord with my whole heart;
 I will tell of all your wonderful deeds.
I will be glad and exult in you;
 I will sing praise to your name, O Most High.

—Psalm 9:1–2

Praise the Lord!
 O give thanks to the Lord, for he is good;
for his steadfast love endures forever.

—Psalm 106:1

Enter his gates with thanksgiving,
and his courts with praise.
 Give thanks to him, bless his name.

—Psalm 100:4

Other Scripture passages you might want to read to express your thanks to God are:

- 1 Chronicles 16:8–36
- Psalm 30

- Psalm 92
- Psalm 111
- Psalm 118
- Psalm 138
- Isaiah 12:1

The unthankful heart... discovers no mercies; but let the thankful heart sweep through the day and, as the magnet finds the iron, so it will find, in every hour, some heavenly blessings!

Henry Ward Beecher

Are you ready to experience and express genuine gratitude to God for restoring you? Whatever healing you have experienced, shouldn't God receive your thanks? Perhaps you have reconciled with an estranged friend or are no longer suffering from arthritis. Your teenager may have come through a difficult period in his or her life. Or you have kicked an addiction that held you prisoner.

~Let Faith Help You Heal~

Such healing doesn't just come out of the blue or by accident. Healing happens when God works in people's lives, though people often credit "medicine," "time," or "my family's support" (all of which are part of God's gifts to us).

Some people keep a special gratitude journal where they record their blessings. If you want to try this, you could choose a blank book that appeals to you (though any format, including typing your gratitude list on the computer, can work). Choose a time each day to reflect on your life. Sit quietly before writing down at least three things for which you are thankful. You can be general (health, friends, family), but the more specific you are (the sound of rain on the roof, Aileen's phone call, that my cold is better) the more you will begin to see how God is at work in your life.

You may be surprised that the more you consciously attune yourself to God's blessings, the more fully you are able to live in thanksgiving and praise. As Teilhard de Chardin said,

Let Faith Help You Heal

"...nothing here below is profane for those who know how to see. On the contrary, everything is sacred..." The gratitude journal helps us focus on the sacred all around us.

Remember how the tenth leper came back to praise God and thank Jesus? Keeping a gratitude journal is one way to remind yourself of how graciously God bestows blessings. Otherwise, many people focus on what is wrong in their lives instead of what is right and good and hopeful.

After writing down those things for which you are grateful, take time to pray, acknowledging God's gifts. If times are hard for you, you can ask for God's help. Perseverance, strength, and patience are necessary and important gifts we all need at different points in our lives.

If the only prayer you said in your whole life was, "thank you," that would suffice.

Meister Eckhart

― Let Faith Help You Heal ―

Do you have any friends or family members who live with such positive outlooks that when you're with them, you can't help but brighten up? Once you tune in to how our heavenly Father is blessing your life, you can be that beacon of light for others, as well. How might you share your gratitude with others to help them work toward their own healing?

Loving Jesus,
Healer of the Sick,
I place in your hands
Myself
And all who need your healing.
Help us crave the healing
That only you can give.
May we not define what that healing should be,
But accept your gift of abundant life
However you give it to us.
In your way, in your time,
Restore us to full health and wholeness.
Amen.

When Muriel, a healthy 72-year-old woman, returned from a camping trip, a friend took one look at her and said, "Your color is off. You should have a doctor check you out."

"I feel fine," Muriel said, but she made the appointment with her family practitioner anyway.

"Something's not right," Muriel's doctor said. "Let's run some tests."

Within days, Muriel's life was turned upside down. Her yellowish skin was an indicator of bile duct cancer. Muriel had a fast-growing cancer for which exploratory surgery showed no cure. The diagnosis? Six to eight weeks to live.

Her family was amazed that even at the moment when the doctor told Muriel that she only had a short time left in this world, she looked only forward without regret.

"I was born into a Christian family," she said. "I have known that God was with me through trials and tribulations in the past. I believe God will see me through this."

"Aren't you going to pray for healing?" one friend asked.

"I've had a good life. I trust God to be with me as long as I live," she said.

Muriel's son desperately wanted healing for her. Just before she passed away, he realized how much healing had come through her illness.

"Because she knew we only had a short time, she didn't waste it on railing against God or feeling sorry for herself. The way she modeled living for us was incredible. Everyone in our family had a chance to spend quality time with her, and it brought all of us close together in a way I hadn't thought possible. So, in an odd way, healing happened even though my mother was not physically healed of her cancer. She had as good a death as anyone could. She died knowing how much she was loved and cherished."

Everyone who knew Muriel felt the impact of her positive spirit and focus on gratitude. Little things they'd been complaining about suddenly seemed not quite as important. Muriel lived fully in the seven weeks between her diagnosis and her death, inspiring others to appreciate their lives and accept their own healing.

Just as I am, thou wilt receive,
Wilt welcome, pardon, cleanse, relieve;
Because thy promise I believe,
O Lamb of God, I come, I come.

Charlotte Elliott

How might you share your gratitude? Begin by completing the following statements:

- I have seen God at work in my life when
_____
_____

- Blessings I have received are
_____
_____

- How I believe God can heal me

  _____

  _____

- God has already healed me by

  _____

  _____

Surely your answers to the above questions contain at least some good news you might share with others. Remember Audrey? Muriel? Others in your own life who have inspired you to look at life with thankful eyes? Proverbs 17:22 (CEV) reminds us how important it is to live with a positive attitude:

> If you are cheerful,
> you feel good;
> if you are sad,
> you hurt all over.

Your experience of healing and your hopeful attitude can encourage someone else to look at their own life differently. Try this simple process for sharing your gratitude in a way that impacts other people's lives:

1. Acknowledge all God has done and is doing in your life.
2. Evaluate gifts you have that might help you help others (personality traits, specific experiences, or other unique things about you).
3. Look at your community, and brainstorm ways in which you can share that gratitude with others.
4. Choose an area of need and take action.
5. Thank God for using you to help others.

This might be as simple as writing letters to someone in prison or attending a support group with a friend who is afraid to go on her own. Every community has a wide variety of people in need. To whom would you feel most comfortable reaching out? Your minister or priest might have some suggestions as to where you could make a difference. Could your gifts best be used at a local school, at shelters for homeless people or abused women, with an individual in your congregation, or at your workplace?

Gracious and Healing God,
Thank you for everything you have done for me in
    the past.
You have restored me in unexpected ways and
I will never be the same.
Thank you for being with me in the present
    and for the bright future you have planned for me.
I pray for those who don't know you yet,
    who don't understand how you bless them again
    and again.
Use me to share the gratitude I feel,
That others may grow to know you and your power.
In the name of Jesus,
Who healed the sick and made the lame to walk,
    I pray.
Amen.

Paul urged Jesus' followers at Philippi to "Rejoice in the Lord always; again I will say, Rejoice. Let your gentleness be known to everyone. The Lord is near. Do not worry about anything, but in everything by prayer and supplication with thanksgiving let your requests be made known to

Let Faith Help You Heal

God. And the peace of God, which surpasses all understanding, will guard your hearts and your minds in Christ Jesus" (Philippians 4:4–7).

J. R. took those words seriously. While in the hospital after a serious car accident, J. R. received visits from the hospital chaplain who not only cheered him up but also challenged him to believe he would recover and be whole again. *What did I have to lose?* J. R. thought. It wasn't easy to "not worry about anything, but in everything by prayer and supplication with thanksgiving let your requests be made known to God." But J. R. determined to call on God for help. "When the going got rough, I repeated these words from Jeremiah 17:14: 'Heal me, O Lord, and I shall be healed; save me, and I shall be saved; for you are my praise.'"

Physical therapy was grueling, but in the therapy room at the hospital, other patients heard J. R. chanting Jeremiah's words. An older woman who had fallen and broken her hip remembers one day when her pain was so great that she felt like giving up. "Then I heard another patient saying under his breath, 'Heal me and I shall be healed.' I decided to stop feeling sorry for myself and get back to work."

And this is the boldness we have in him, that if we ask anything according to his will, he hears us. And if we know that he hears us in whatever we ask, we know that we have obtained the requests made of him.

1 John 5:14–15

Who knows whose life might be changed because we dare to share our gratitude for God's healing in our lives? If, as Henry Ward Beecher said, "Gratitude is the fairest blossom which springs from the soul," then isn't it time for your spirit of thankfulness to blossom in the world?

―Let Faith Help You Heal―

Focus on an Intimate and Vibrant Relationship with God

*We are not human beings having
a spiritual experience.*

*We are spiritual beings having
a human experience.*

Teilhard de Chardin

Have you ever learned a new vocabulary word, only to discover that the word pops up in books, conversations, or on the news? Similarly, when we pay attention to what God has done and is doing in our lives, we suddenly realize how very present God is in many aspects of our lives. Now that you've considered some of the ways God may be present in your life, offering you healing and new life, wouldn't you like to stay close to God?

Let Faith Help You Heal

Our desire to know God springs from our own need for connection. As wonderful as it is when we can surround ourselves with people who love us, there is in us a thirst for the holy that earthly people and things cannot fill. No human can love us in the same way God loves us. As the psalmist said,

O God, you are my God, I seek you,
   my soul thirsts for you;
my flesh faints for you,
   as in a dry and weary land where there is no water.

—Psalm 63:1

To repeat Augustine's passionate words: "Our hearts are restless until they find their rest in God." We are most complete when we fill the empty places inside us with God's Spirit. Our healing will most clearly continue if we develop devotional practices and spiritual disciplines that keep us close to God and still our restless hearts.

In the 17th century, a French Carmelite monk named Brother Lawrence of the Resurrection developed a rich spiritual life based on what he called "The Practice of the Presence of God." Brother Lawrence said, "The time of business is no different from the time of prayer. In the noise and clatter of my kitchen, I possess God as tranquilly as if I were upon my knees before the Blessed Sacrament."

*Nothing true or beautiful or good
Makes complete sense in any immediate
context of history;
Therefore we must be saved by faith.*

Reinhold Neibuhr

Don't you love the image of Brother Lawrence communing with God as he scrubs the pots and pans? In a letter he wrote to a religious woman, Brother Lawrence said, "In the midst of your work, console yourself with God as often as you can. During your meals and your conversations, lift your hearts toward God from time to time…

To do this you need not shout out loud. God is closer than we think. We do not have to be constantly in church to be with God. We can make our heart a prayer room into which we can retire from time to time to converse with God gently, humbly and lovingly."

This simply means remembering that God is with us in the present moment. Whether we are preparing dinner, standing in line at the post office, visiting someone in the hospital, washing dishes, or feeling frustrated because the battery in our car is dead, God is with us. For some of us, God is most powerfully experienced in the grandeur of nature. Others are especially reminded of their Creator by holding the hand of a small child, watching the gradual transformation of another person's life, or experiencing a new understanding from hearing a sermon or reading a book.

We often meet God when we least expect it. We may be intent on a task or wrapped up in our own agenda, then, as Blanche DuBois says in *A*

Streetcar Named Desire, "Sometimes there's God, so quickly."

Moses experienced "God, so quickly" when he was taken aback by the burning bush: "Moses was keeping the flock of his father-in-law Jethro, the priest of Midian; he led his flock beyond the wilderness, and came to Horeb, the mountain of God. There the angel of the Lord appeared to him in a flame of fire out of a bush; he looked, and the bush was blazing, yet it was not consumed. Then Moses said, 'I must turn aside and look at this great sight, and see why the bush is not burned up.' When the Lord saw that he had turned aside to see, God called to him out of the bush, 'Moses, Moses!' And he said, 'Here I am.' Then he said, 'Come no closer! Remove the sandals from your feet, for the place on which you are standing is holy ground.' He said further, 'I am the God of your father, the God of Abraham, the God of Isaac, and the God of Jacob.' And Moses hid his face, for he was afraid to look at God" (Exodus 3:1–6).

─Let Faith Help You Heal─

God may not speak to you from a bush, but if you are open to God's presence in your life, you will feel God's presence as you pray or read Scripture or converse with another person. We can always "practice the presence of God," no matter where or when or how. We always stand on holy ground.

I could not say I believe, I know!
I have had the experience of being gripped
by something that is stronger than myself,
Something that people call God.

Carl Jung

As Christians, we know that lives can be changed, healed, made new in Jesus. We also know that becoming Christian is not a matter of "I believe" and then going back to life a usual. We should always be growing in faith. As Methodist founder John Wesley said, we "are going on to Perfection." So how do we grow in our faith and continue to come closer to the One who heals us?

Some people see the spiritual life as a ladder: God is "up there in heaven," and we're down here on earth. Step by step, we can reach God in a sort of "We Are Climbing Jacob's Ladder Toward God" process. With that idea, the higher we go, the better we are; the more we do (Bible study, prayer group, fasting), the further ahead of others we are on the spiritual path.

Although we may admire those who spend hours each day on their knees praying, such devotion doesn't work for everyone. Sometimes we are daunted by the examples of other Christians who seem to be "more spiritual" and "holier" than we know ourselves to be. A life of faith is not a competition for the Most Spiritual award; we don't sign up for Faith 101, a course we must pass before we go on to the next level.

Each of us can develop our personal "lifetime spirituality" that informs how we live through all the ages and stages of our lives. A lifetime of spirituality takes into account:

Let Faith Help You Heal

- who we are
- who we understand God to be
- our routines and responsibilities
- our willingness to make time for God

God enters by a private door into every individual.

Ralph Waldo Emerson

Before we explore what devotional practices and spiritual disciplines will keep you connected to God, take time to reflect on your relationship with God:

When I was a child, I pictured God as

_____

_____

As a teenager, God was for me

_____

_____

Now, when I think of God, I feel
_____
_____

If I were to draw a picture of God, God might look like
_____
_____

These words describe God for me:
___ powerful
___ all-knowing
___ silent
___ vengeful
___ punishing
___ a good listener
___ the giver of life
___ omniscient
___ inaccessible
___ just
___ mysterious
___ peaceful
___ patient
___ gentle
___ invisible
___ loving
___ forgiving
___ ever-present
___ controlling
___ nurturing
___ immortal
___ understanding
___ gracious
___ eternal
___ tender
___ forceful

― Let Faith Help You Heal ―

___ frightening   ___ righteous
___ wise   ___ angry
___ immortal   ___ comforting
___ just   ___ creative
___ persistent   ___ merciful

If I were to describe my relationship with God, I would say

_____

_____

_____

*More things are wrought by prayer
Than this world dreams of.*

Alfred, Lord Tennyson

Prayer is the heart of the human/divine relationship. As in any relationship, the more time we spend with God, the better we know each other. Prayer is not just a monologue where we list all the wants and the needs we hope God will fill. Prayer is also listening, giving God time to speak to us, being open to the various ways God may speak: through other humans, through our dreams, through a strong instinct or moment of conscience.

Faced with a career decision that would alter the direction of her future, Addie prayed, "I'm confused about what to do next. Please lead me in the right direction." The next day she felt a strong sense that one choice was the best. "It was another week before I remembered my prayer, though," she admits, "and realized my prayer had been answered."

Some people find it helpful to write down their prayer requests so they can go back to the list and recognize answers to their prayers. Other people join prayer groups to intercede for others' needs. All of us benefit when we set aside regular times to communicate with God—both speaking and listening.

The Bible contains the record of how God acted at many points in human history. We see how other human beings related to God, and we learn from their experiences even if they lived centuries before us. We find law, history, prophecy, and poetry in the 39 books of the Old Testament (also known as the Hebrew Scripture), but, most importantly, this first testament of the Bible details God's relationship with the chosen people, the Hebrews.

Our prayer will be most like the prayer of Christ if we do not ask God to show us what is going to be, or to make any particular thing happen, but only pray that we may be faithful in whatever happens.

Father Andrew

The New Testament's 27 books contain four Gospels telling the story of Jesus' life, ministry, death, and resurrection; the history of the early church (Acts of the Apostles); letters between church leaders and people in various congregations; and Revelation, a book about the end times.

The Bible is the story of God's great love for God's people across the centuries. You can read its pages on your own or in a group, but you'll be amazed at how much you can learn about your own heart in its pages. The psalmist makes this very point: "Your word is a lamp to my feet and a light to my path" (Psalm 119:105). If reading Scripture is new to you, you might want to start with one of the Gospels, each telling the story of the Lord and Savior Jesus.

*When you read God's word,
you must constantly be saying to yourself,
"It is talking to me, and about me."*

Søren Kierkegaard

Numerous devotional books can guide you and add to your understanding as you read the Bible. Whatever method you choose as you spend time with God's Word, you may soon agree with Ernest Hellos's assessment of the Bible: "It is impossible to explain how profound it is, impossible to explain how simple it is."

Worship is another key way we stay close to God. Whether we are in awe of the glories of creation ("How great thou art!") or feeling a strong sense of community at a church service, worship is our chance to "keep the Sabbath holy," giving thanks and praise to God. "The church as a worshiping community carries our biblical faith and spiritual tradition down through the ages to each individual," says Marjorie Thompson. There is something powerful about gathering with other believers and proclaiming the mysteries of faith.

You may already have a church home. If not, you may want to visit different churches in your community to see where you feel the most at home since wide styles of worship exist. You may prefer a more formal, traditional service. Or a relaxed, contemporary worship may fit you better. What is important is that you make time to focus on who God is and what God has done and is doing in your life and the life of your faith community.

To worship is to quicken the conscience by the Holiness of God
To feed the mind with the Truth of God
To purge the imagination by the Beauty of God
To devote the will to the Purpose of God.

William Temple

Other ways you might choose to strengthen your relationship with God include:

- spiritual or devotional reading (contemporary or classic religious literature);
- listening to religious music;
- meditation (quiet time focused on God);
- devotional groups;
- attending educational opportunities offered by your church;

- working with a spiritual director (a religious guide);
- going on a personal retreat (time apart to focus on God);
- fasting (from food, shopping, negative remarks, television, or anything that gets in the way of our relationship with God);
- spiritual friendship (sharing your faith journey with another person).

Any way you choose to focus on and connect with God will help you continue your process of healing and fulfill your Healing Vision Statement. Relationship with God is a gift that is offered to us without price. Believing in God is a lifelong process.

God with me lying down,
God with me rising up,
God with me in each ray of light,
Nor I a ray of joy without Him,
Nor one ray without Him.

Christ with me sleeping,
Christ with me waking,

> **Christ with me watching,**
> **Every day and night,**
> **Each day and night.**
> **God with me protecting,**
> **The Lord with me directing,**
> **The Spirit with me strengthening,**
> **For ever and for evermore,**
> **Ever and evermore,**
> **Amen.**
>
> —Celtic Prayer

We should always be growing in our spirituality: the ways we act out our faith in Jesus Christ and continue to be formed by God.

Even those who knew Jesus personally had trouble recognizing the Risen Christ. Remember how on Easter Sunday two of the disciples were walking to Emmaus when Jesus joined them?

"While they were talking and discussing, Jesus himself came near and went with them, but their eyes were kept from recognizing him. And he said to them, 'What are you discussing with each other while you walk along?' They stood still, looking sad. Then one of them, whose name was Cleopas, answered him, 'Are you the only stranger in Jerusalem who does not know the things that have taken place there in these days?'" (Luke 24:15–18).

The men conveyed to Jesus all that happened surrounding the recent death of their Lord. They were so wrapped up in their own grief that they didn't even know who he was when "beginning with Moses and all the prophets, he interpreted to them the things about himself in all the scriptures.

"As they came near the village to which they were going, he walked ahead as if he were going on. But they urged him strongly, saying, 'Stay with us, because it is almost evening and the day is now nearly over.' So he went in to stay with them. When he was at the table with them, he took bread, blessed and broke it, and gave it to them. Then their eyes were opened, and they recognized him; and he vanished from their sight. They said to each other, 'Were not our hearts burning within us while he was talking to us on the road, while he was opening the scriptures to us?' That same hour they got up and returned to Jerusalem; and they found the eleven and their companions gathered together. They were saying, 'The Lord has risen indeed, and he has appeared to Simon!' Then they told what had happened on the road, and how he had been made known to them in the breaking of the bread" (verses 27–35).

Even those of us who have felt Jesus' healing touch sometimes need to be reminded of who he is. Our daily routines may blind us to his power. By choosing spiritual disciplines and devotional practices, however, and by focusing our gaze on what God is doing in our lives, our healing will continue as long as we live.

Expect great things from God.
Attempt great things for God.

William Carey

Let Faith Help You Heal

Be assured that God is working in your life. The more you give yourself over to the spiritual life, the more you will realize God's power and feel connected to God's love. Wholeness, healing, health—all these are possible if you believe in God's power to heal, envision yourself whole, learn to forgive, and allow God to transform your life. Once you let go of that which binds you, you can reach out to others as a wounded healer, thanking God for your new life and helping others work toward their healing.

God loves you and wants to know you and be in a relationship with you. An intimate and vibrant relationship with God *is* possible if you seek God and claim the new life God offers.